# 10 AIRPORTS

## Fentress Bradburn Architects

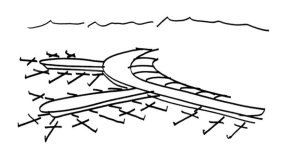

EDIZIONI

5

*Previous page:* Sketch of JCN by Curtis Worth Fentress
*Left:* South-end curtainwall at DEN

# The Next Generation of Airport Design

By Curtis Worth Fentress, FAIA

Airports are monumental portals—gateways to communities, countries, and adventures. As the world has become smaller through technological, political, economic, and social metamorphoses, passenger terminals have become civic buildings. Along with being designated "civic" facilities comes profound responsibility: to promote a greater sense of humanity by representing the culture, geography, and human spirit in which they are rooted.

The ten terminals in this book are among the first in the world to realize civic responsibility. In them, you will see the power of civic-minded airport design to stir one's soul and ignite the prowess of an entire community. Each example is an iteration of Contextual Regionalism, our firm's design philosophy. This approach unearths the unique combination of elements that define a site, and, thus, the building upon it. An area's history, culture, memory, and myth are evoked in form-giving solutions that operate on metaphor, symbol, and even legend. Making these abstract concepts material is the ongoing challenge that sustains us through the natural—albeit often protracted—process of creating public spaces. Yet the look of a terminal is only half the equation.

The other guiding factor in civic-minded airport design is the feel of a space, or the experience of passage. Because of their purpose and designation as civic facilities, terminals demand a dramatic sense of arrival and delivery to the passenger's ultimate destination. While in English the word "passage" is traditionally understood as the movement from point A to point B, civic airports should embody its Latin root *passus,* which is decidedly more than that. The varied and colorful connotations of *passus* may best be distilled down to a single concept: the creation of a moment or a series of them.

Over the last 25 years, we have nurtured a rhythm to evoke and intermingle these two essentials: look and feel. The rhythm is based on intelligence, tempered by experience, and guided by intuition. We begin with a master plan and then work through the departure and arrival sequences. At each stage, at every level, we seek to create spaces that will impart an aura of dignity, warmth, and welcome for decades to come. ■

*Left:* Retail esplanade at SEA
*Following page:* Jet bridges at JCN

# DEN

Passenger Terminal Complex
Denver International Airport

| | |
|---|---|
| location | Denver, Colorado, USA |
| conditions | new construction, Greenfield site |
| type | multi-airline hub, O&D |
| area | 2,250,000 sqft (185,800 sqm)<br>*UD: 4,250,000 sqft (395,000 sqm)* |
| annual pax | 55 million at capacity<br>*UD: 110 million* |
| gates | 94 attached<br>*UD: 124* |
| scope | programming, planning,<br>design, & construction |

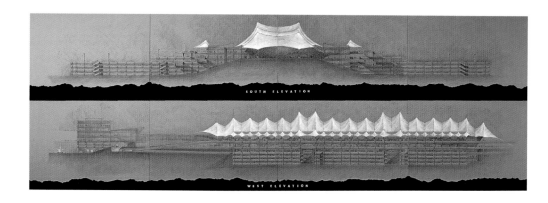

SOUTH ELEVATION

WEST ELEVATION

*Previous page:*
Peaked roofline with
the Rocky Mountains

*Top:*
South and west
elevations

*Right:*
Aerial with
concourses beyond

*Facing page left:*
Rocky Mountain peak

*Facing page right:*
Denver skyline

## Master Plan

Announced in 1985 as the replacement for land-starved Stapleton Airport, DEN was the answer to the city's growing demand for air transportation, the resolution to national congestion issues caused by runway sequencing in inclement weather, and the means to establish an internationally-recognized landmark for the region. With a 53-square-mile (85-square-kilometer) plot of land 45 minutes from downtown Denver, then-mayor Federico Peña approved a master plan that called for one terminal, five concourses, nearly 400 gates, 12 runways, 24,000 parking spaces, light rail access, and the capacity to serve 110 million passengers annually. While the opening in 1995 introduced less than half of the planned facilities, this forward-looking airport continues to serve as a benchmark for its contemporaries around the world.

Many innovative strategies were implemented in the design of this airport. The terminal's unique plan is essentially a linear terminal folded back on itself. This created a clear span Great Hall that minimizes walking distances to the centrally located APM, which is accessed by either of two security checkpoints. With three levels of vehicular access on both sides of the building, this terminal configuration cuts congestion along the curbside that lines the 1,000-foot-long (305-meter-long) building. Of its 5,400 feet (1,646 meters), 1,800 linear feet (549 meters) are dedicated to each of the following: non-commercial arrivals, commercial arrivals and departures, and non-commercial departures. Parking structures, adjacent to each curbside, were carved out of the landscape to give ticketing and baggage levels unobstructed views to the mountains and plains.

## Concept

As Frank Lloyd Wright heralded, "Form follows function—that has been misunderstood. Form and function should be one, joined in a spiritual union." Because of the foresight and leadership of individuals like Peña and then-director Bill Smith, Denver International Airport is at once a memorable gateway and a practical solution.

The terminal's design draws inspiration from its breathtaking backdrop and the abundant sunshine that the site's high plains desert environment bestows upon the building. Initial design concepts investigated the best means to incorporate natural light and mimic the angular nature of the majestic Rocky Mountains. Extensive study involving a series of models yielded the conclusion that a fabric roof, rather than a traditional one, would not only better express the design goals, it would be easier to maintain and quicker to construct.

The combination of a solid, earth-toned base with a soaring, light-filled roofing material speaks to the confluence of mountains and plains, the intersection of land and air, and the magic of flight. Similarly, the combination of an efficient operational design with an aesthetic vision and innovative building technologies celebrates progress and achievement while enabling the airport to achieve a timeless, enduring quality.

*Below left:* Aerial
*Below right:* Ticket counter
*Right:* Departure curbside approach

14

## Landside Experience

Most departing passengers arrive via the dedicated boulevard named for the airport's principal champion: Federico Peña. Whether arriving by car, bus, or the soon-to-be-added light rail line, passengers glimpse the terminal's roof from sightlines now guarded by law. Once inside the airport's spacious property, ample signage directs passengers to car rental returns, holding lots for meeters and greeters, parking, and airline-specific drop-off zones. Departing passengers being dropped off by taxis and personal vehicles are directed to the top tier of a three-tiered curb system. Here, curbside canopies line 900 linear feet (274 meters) on both sides of the terminal to provide shelter for embarking passengers. The fabric canopies reinforce the building's contextually inspired design as they mirror the larger peaks that rise above the great hall.

## Ticketing

The top tier of the curbside system provides immediate access to the ticketing halls, which span column-free the full length of both the eastern and western sides of the terminal. Inside, daylight washes the space while granite floor patterns, reminiscent of the peaked roof, guide passengers toward ticketing counters and then on to the Great Hall.

Passengers arriving by commercial vehicle or as part of a charter group arrive one floor down. Pre-ticketed and curbside ticketed passengers proceed directly into the Great Hall where they find concessions and security.

## Great Hall

Over 25 million of the more than 42 million passengers that passed through DEN in 2004 experienced the Great Hall space. The remaining 17 million were transfer passengers. The south end's curtainwall measures 220 feet (67 meters) wide by 60 feet (18 meters) tall and offers panoramic views to the Rocky Mountains' Pikes Peak and downtown Denver.

The massing of the Great Hall, which rises like the barrel-vaulted roofs of Manhattan's Grand Central Station and Washington, DC's Union Station, encourages a moment of repose. Whether entering from ticketing or baggage claim, travelers are at once oriented to the concessions that line both levels, to the two bridges that traverse the space connecting the eastern and western ticketing halls, and to the north and south security checkpoints.

## Interior Materials

Earth-toned peaks of granite direct passengers into the ticketing area and recall the peaks of the mountain-inspired roof. Inside the Great Hall, browns, blues, and greens dot the floor in an abstract pattern reminiscent of an aerial perspective of the eastern Colorado agrarian landscape. The train platform's narrowing circles of blue draw people in to the space, making room for additional passengers. Baggage claim features the same pattern as ticketing, only in reverse, as it channels passengers out to awaiting taxis and vans or down a level to the personal vehicle pick-up area. Brushed stainless steel clads column bases, elevator jambs, and doors, as well as lower portions of the ticketing counters, to mask the inevitable scarring caused by baggage carts, cleaning equipment, and more. Easy-to-replace carpet squares are another mainstay of the design that augments the facility's durability and longevity.

## Retail

The same guiding force is at work in the Great Hall of the terminal as in Denver's highly successful 16th Street Pedestrian Mall or the great piazzas of Italy. Passengers need not seek out a destination because destinations fall along any one of the designated routes that a passenger takes from check-in to security. Likewise, since the Great Hall also receives all arriving passengers, they, too, are introduced to the hall's numerous services.

## Security & Train

Security was consciously divided into two areas in order to minimize walking distances, reduce security queues, and disperse departing passengers along the APM station platform. Ample pre-security lounge space constitutes both ends of the hall, and was designed to maintain an open environment even in the wake of reoriented and expanded security checkpoints. Potted plants, museum exhibits, carpet, and unencumbered views to the actual screening point help create as comfortable and transparent a process as possible. Once screened, passengers descend one level via stairways, escalators, and elevators from either security checkpoint to a central APM platform that serves each of the remote island concourses. An around-the-world clock and classic modern interiors play up the urban nature of this underground train station.

*Facing page:* Great Hall
*Below:* South-end curtainwall

## Structural Materials

The terminal has one of the largest structurally integrated tensile membrane roofs in the world. Coupled with its striking roof structure, the sheer magnitude of the building captivates travelers as they approach from both land and air.

The translucent roof is, technically speaking, a tensile membrane structure consisting of a Teflon-coated fiberglass membrane reinforced by high-strength steel cables. Two rows of steel masts, 150 feet (46 meters) apart and spaced at 60-foot (18-meter) intervals, support the lightweight roof in an arrangement similar to that of the columns in a large-span suspension bridge. The roof structure, supported by 28 masts reaching up to 150 feet (46 meters) tall, can safely shift up to two feet (just less than a meter) at peak points during high wind storms.

Although the roof generated some skepticism, in actuality the structure is rated by roofing experts to perform better than conventional roofing systems for spans greater than 100 feet (30 meters). The fabric weighs two pounds per square foot less than traditional roofing materials, allows stratified hot air to escape by radiating out through the fabric and, due to its translucency, minimizes the need for artificial lighting. In turn, reduced lighting loads lessens energy consumption and heat production. Further reduction of heat transfer and build up is eliminated through the roof's ability to reflect 40 percent of incident solar radiation.

## Lighting

With an average of 300 days of sunshine per year, careful consideration was given to ensure that the airport would exude a humanized sense of calm and comfort. Even on overcast days, the interior space is washed with natural light from an abundance of clerestories, a curtainwall, and the translucent roof. At night, the roof emits a soft glow and becomes a beacon on the plains as the sun sets beyond the mountains.

19

*Left:* Roof overhang and patio off south end
*Right:* Sketch by Curtis Worth Fentress
*Below:* West side with parking garage uplit at night

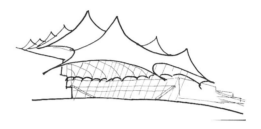

### Train Arrival

Passengers arriving to the terminal from one of the outlying concourses disembark onto APM platforms before ascending by way of escalators and elevators to the Great Hall. A series of folded metal *Paper Airplanes,* part of the airport's extensive art program, hover above the escalators to reinforce the already intuitive arrivals procession. In fact, the planes helped inform the interior design by inspiring the mountain-like granite cladding on the walls.

### Public Art

The unique fusion of art and architecture at DEN is one of the key attributes that sets this facility apart from its contemporaries. Design team members, airport operators, and civic leaders collaborated during the early planning phases to evaluate locations and recommend a shortlist of artists based on portfolios submitted.

As one of the world's largest integrated art programs, DEN is host to 26 permanent sculptures, murals, and installations. These works of art not only enhance the overall aesthetics, they also enhance the airport's functionality, acoustics, and maintainability.

In addition to *Paper Airplanes,* (see Train Arrival) the terminal houses the water sculpture *Mountain Mirage,* the mural *America, Why I Love Her,* and the light art sculpture *Skydance,* among others. One percent of the construction budget was set aside to fund DEN's public art program.

### Baggage Claim

Located directly below each airline's corresponding ticket counters on both sides of the building are the baggage claim areas. The areas immediately surrounding each of the 18 carousels are carpeted to reduce noise and provide less rigid surfaces for standing patrons. Coffered ceiling tiles and indirect lighting help animate and heighten the space. Walkways are designated with the same granite patterns as ticketing, only in reverse, to lead patrons out to awaiting taxis.

Arriving passengers being picked up by personal vehicles are directed to the lowest of the three-level curbside. Commercial vehicle pick-up and drop-off areas are located at the middle level of the three-tiered curbside, which is also the baggage claim and passenger security screening level.

*Left:*
South-end elevation lit from within

*Right:*
Train arrival platform with artwork

Baggage Information

Terminal East
Baggage Claim, Ticketing/Check-in
Ground Transportation

## Security

Stemming from the tragic events of September 11, 2001, the TSA and the U.S. Department of Homeland Security mandated fundamental changes to security processing at every commercial airport in America. More detailed processing translated into longer queue lines, greater amounts of belt-screened items, bomb-detection units, privacy rooms for those needing additional screening, and, most notably, composure areas for people to reassemble belongings. Given the flexibility afforded by the design of the Great Hall, DEN's two existing security checkpoints were able to expand. Only half of the lounge area located at either end of the terminal was needed to accommodate this expansion.

An additional eight screening stations were added to each side, bringing the total number to 20. In addition to the updated magnetometers, belt screening counters were elongated on either side of x-ray machines and rollers were added to speed the process. Fully enclosed secondary screening rooms made of glass were added to allow passengers to maintain a direct line of sight to their items at all times, and special-needs stations were also added to each checkpoint. These critical security upgrades were integrated during continuous operation of what has become the tenth busiest airport in the world.

## Concourse A – RJ Facility Expansion

Frontier, JetExpress, Horizon, and Great Lakes Airlines struggled to accommodate their ever-expanding passenger loads out of the pre-existing 13 gates that were nestled along the narrow commuter portion of Concourse A. This, combined with the growing dependence of domestic airlines on RJs, precipitated DEN to upgrade and expand its RJ facilities.

The 5,200-square-foot (1,585-square-meter) expansion to the eastern end of Concourse A provides over 2,100 square feet (640 square meters) of seating for up to 140 passengers; 1,700 square feet (518 square meters) of circulation; three new gates (one relocated gate); two additional gate counters; two restrooms; and two airline offices. The expansion also addressed upgrades to building systems along the entire length of the commuter facility to enhance passengers' climate comfort.

Similar interior finishes and architectural elements seamlessly meld with the concourse's established architectural vernacular. And, given this opportunity for expansion, designers outfitted the facility with even greater capacity for additional expansion and reconfiguration possibilities.

23

*Facing page:* Expanded security checkpoints
*Below:* Floor plan of Concourse A's expanded regional jet facility

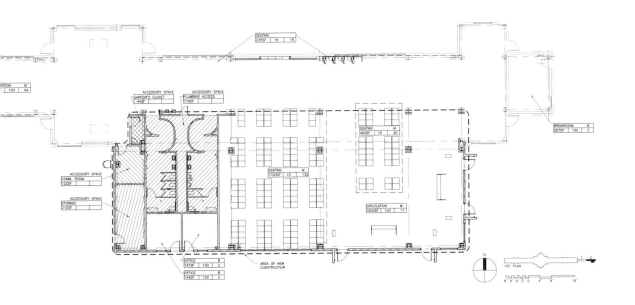

24

### AirTrain

Expansion to the East Corridor of Denver's Light Rail line is a $701 million component of the $4.7 billion FasTracks ballot initiative that local residents approved in November 2004. The East Corridor will link downtown, Stapleton, and Denver International Airport with six new rail stations spread along 23 miles of new rail line. While a train station at Denver International Airport was a consideration in the original design for the main terminal, Fentress Bradburn was engaged to conduct further planning and feasibility studies based on FasTracks' updated 12-year vision.

Studies have focused on creating a new platform at the south end of the terminal to receive arriving passengers and an adjacent platform to stage departing passengers who are awaiting the next train. Additional planning, programming, and design considerations focus on passenger circulation to ticketing, retail, and security, and from the intra-airport APMs and baggage claim.

### FIDs & BIDs

In addition to the upgrades associated with FasTracks and security, continued growth at Denver International Airport has spawned a number of typical upgrade projects, including the retrofit of its FIDs & BIDs. With ten years of heavy use and operation under their belt, airport operators elected to replace the original CRT system with larger LED monitors. The ability to project larger font types allows passengers to read the information from greater distances with increased accuracy. Additionally, the design of the LED system is more in line with the image of the terminal; their brushed stainless steel bases match existing cladding on columns, and their clean lines and black frames complement the signage program.

### FIS Expansion

DEN now processes millions more annual international arrivals than it did when the airport opened just a decade ago. Given the constrained capacity and a projected increase in passenger numbers, DEN's operators made the easy decision to upgrade the FIS facility. In addition to increasing baggage claim capacity by 33 percent, operators also used this opportunity to bring the facility into compliance with new CBP regulations, as well as to enhance and update its design.

The new design is a modern complement to the interiors of the terminal, which were inspired by aerial photographs of the local landscape including mountains, crop fields, and riverbeds. Rich red and earth-toned carpets are accompanied by natural granites in similar hues. The contrasting stainless steel finish on the baggage carousels and black metal frames of the BIDs add sophistication and elegance. Additional lighting in the facility not only primes passengers for the warmly daylit interior of the terminal, it also creates a more effective environment for the departments at work inside, which includes CBP, PHS, and USFWS.

# BKK

Terminal & Concourses
Second Bangkok International Airport

| | |
|---|---|
| location | Bangkok, Thailand |
| conditions | new construction, Greenfield site |
| type | multi-airline hub, O&D |
| area | 5,000,000 sqft (501,600 sqm)<br>*UD: 16,200,000 sqft (1,505,000 sqm)* |
| annual pax | 30 million at capacity<br>*UD: 100 million* |
| gates | 46 attached<br>*UD: 108* |
| scope | design competition entry |

## Master Plan

The program for BKK called for a four-story replacement terminal situated between parallel runways. In addition to being constrained, this site possessed a high water table. Sixteen alternate site configurations were developed by Fentress Bradburn's design team during the international design competition as a means to further study the site. Each configuration was evaluated on passenger convenience, airport operation, and economy of cost and construction.

The ideal configuration was determined to be a linear passenger terminal with two concourses: one attached and one remote. Additional elements in the integrated complex include elevated frontage roads, a vehicular parking structure, integrated offices, operational support facilities, and provision for future rail access.

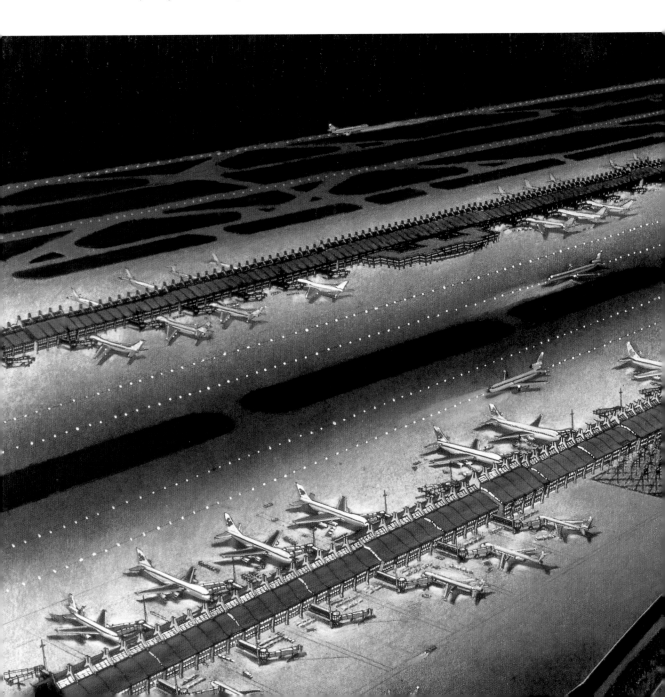

## Phasing

The terminal and concourses can be erected in five phases. The first four phases consist of erecting modules that each process 7.5 million annual passengers with the requisite baggage handling, ticketing, and gate facilities. Modularization not only allows the airport to be operational quickly, it provides a means for manageable growth and a repetition of building materials, which reduce costs. The final phase, module five, contains the retail and office space, as well as a "meeters and greeters" hall that connects all public levels.

*Previous page:* Curbside approach with concourse on left
*Below:* Aerial illustrating ultimate development

*Below:* Model of curbside approach
*Facing page top:* Section model of terminal
*Facing page middle:* Royal Barge
*Facing page bottom:* Traditional palace architecture

30

## Landside Departure Experience

From the exterior through the interior, the design comes alive with symbolism. The approach roads and surrounding land are designed with densely planted grasses, shrubs, trees, and lush flower gardens, rich and magnificent in color. Approaching the terminal, the landscape transitions from groves to hardwood savannah, found in northern Thailand. At the final approach, draping bougainvillea and flowering vines are layered along the terraced walls, while palms and bamboo arch outward from the terraces to create a floral portal, signaling arrival at the terminal.

## Ticketing

Over the past few decades, Thailand has progressed into the global marketplaces of trade, commerce, and tourism. The design of the ticketing hall captures this progress in the structural technology used to create visual interpretations of Thailand's rich heritage. The Royal Barge served as inspiration for the hall's roof form; its curvilinear lines and ribbed structure recall the barge's hull and establish the foundation for the long-span structure. The same three-dimensional truss system is replicated a level below to introduce clerestories that allow natural light deep into the hall without the use of skylights, which are vulnerable to tropical monsoons.

The design team further maximized the long-term flexibility of this space by placing columns along the perimeter. This allows the flexible interior to be rearranged to accommodate future advancements in passenger check-in procedures.

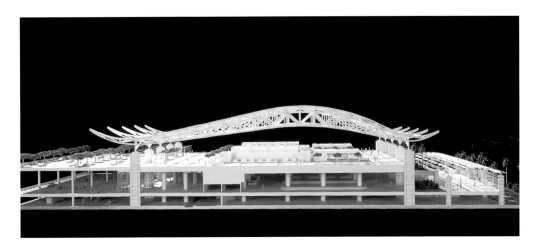

*Facing page top:* Landscaping between terminal and concourse
*Facing page bottom:* Section model of concourse and terminal
*Below:* Rice paddies

## Landscaping

Historically, landscape planning and gardening has played a large role in the design of important places in Bangkok and Thailand. The major palaces of Thailand are, in fact, large complexes of buildings set in lavish gardens. These gardens are more than quiet, reflective spaces; they are spaces literally alive with tradition and symbolism. The design for BKK incorporates significant landscaping both on the exterior and within the complex: buildings inside gardens and gardens inside buildings.

34

## Airside Arrival Experience

An abstract lotus motif forms the concourse roofline. At the base of the lotus form, the roof sweeps out, recalling traditional and unique Thai roof forms and the image of aircraft lift-off.

Inside, the design was inspired by the "Four Great Essentials" of Buddhism: earth, water, fire, and air. "Earth" inspired the design of the landside terminal; the solid and earth-toned space has a grounding effect on arriving and departing passengers alike. "Water" inspired the circulation patterns throughout the airport complex; fluid and adaptable in nature, these paths move passengers quickly and efficiently. "Fire," perhaps the most difficult element to represent because it is defined as energy, was a guiding factor throughout; from furnishings to finishes, all materials were designed to convey vivacity and maturity. "Air" inspired the concourses; peaked and light in color, the concourses prepare passengers for flight and movement.

The strong and clearly defined vision for the interiors supports the overall focus on passenger comfort and convenience. Color coding, clear circulation lines, and changes in ceiling elevation serve to strengthen passengers' orientation at all points along their journey.

Due to the concourse's extreme length, dictated by site constraints, the design provides for the addition of an above-grade APM at any point during development. The APM would greatly reduce connection times for hubbing passengers needing to get from one end of the concourse to the other.

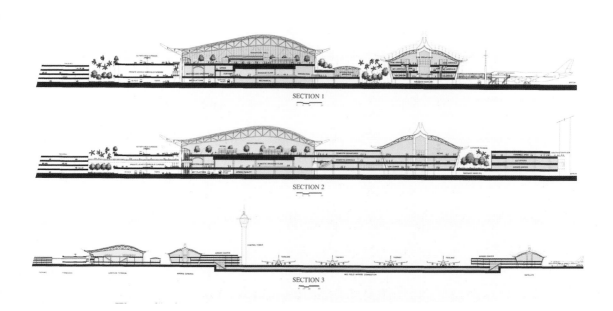

SECTION 1

SECTION 2

SECTION 3

# DOH

Terminal & Concourse,
Support Buildings, Control Tower
Doha International Airport

| | |
|---|---|
| location | Doha, Qatar |
| conditions | expansion, renovation & new construction, Green and Brownfield site |
| type | single-airline hub, O&D |
| area | terminal & concourse: 900,000 sqft (83,600 sqm) support buildings: 166,000 sqft (15,400 sqm) control tower: 77,500 sqft (7,200 sqm) |
| annual pax | 10 million at capacity |
| gates | 20 attached |
| scope | terminal & concourse, control tower: programming, planning, & design support buildings: programming, planning, design, & construction |

**Phased Development**

In order to meet passenger and freight growth forecasts through 2020 and beyond, Qatar's Ministry of Municipal Affairs and Agriculture embarked on a major facilities expansion program. The Ministry conducted an international design competition in 1996 for DOH's architect, from which Fentress Bradburn emerged as the unanimous winner.

Over the course of several years, the firm was retained to complete the design of three components for DOH. The first project completed was Component I: the relocation and upgrade of numerous support facilities including a control tower, fire station, and fuel farm. Relocation of these facilities cleared the site intended for a replacement passenger terminal complex. This terminal complex,

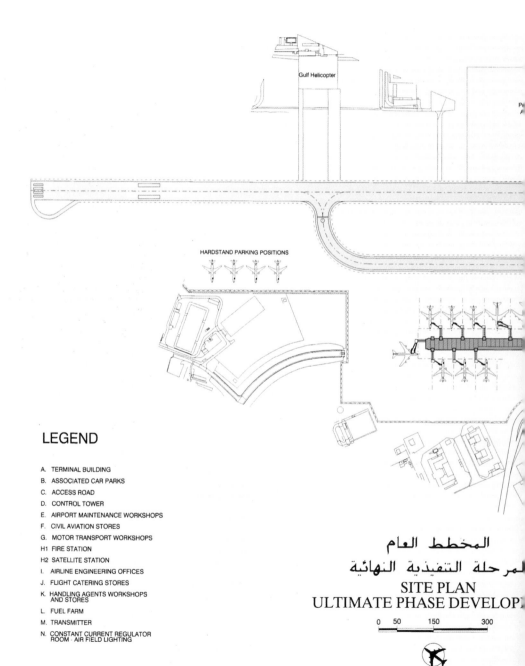

LEGEND

A.  TERMINAL BUILDING
B.  ASSOCIATED CAR PARKS
C.  ACCESS ROAD
D.  CONTROL TOWER
E.  AIRPORT MAINTENANCE WORKSHOPS
F.  CIVIL AVIATION STORES
G.  MOTOR TRANSPORT WORKSHOPS
H1  FIRE STATION
H2  SATELLITE STATION
I.  AIRLINE ENGINEERING OFFICES
J.  FLIGHT CATERING STORES
K.  HANDLING AGENTS WORKSHOPS
    AND STORES
L.  FUEL FARM
M.  TRANSMITTER
N.  CONSTANT CURRENT REGULATOR
    ROOM : AIR FIELD LIGHTING

المخطط العام
المرحلة التنفيذية النهائية
SITE PLAN
ULTIMATE PHASE DEVELOP

0    50    150    300

also known as Component II, went through several iterations based on an evolving set of criteria driven by the Ministry, a growing local economy, and the advent of new airline hubbing operations. Component III, a 290-foot-tall (90-meter-tall) control tower, was precipitated by the addition of a second runway, and unites the entire complex in a cohesive architectural statement.

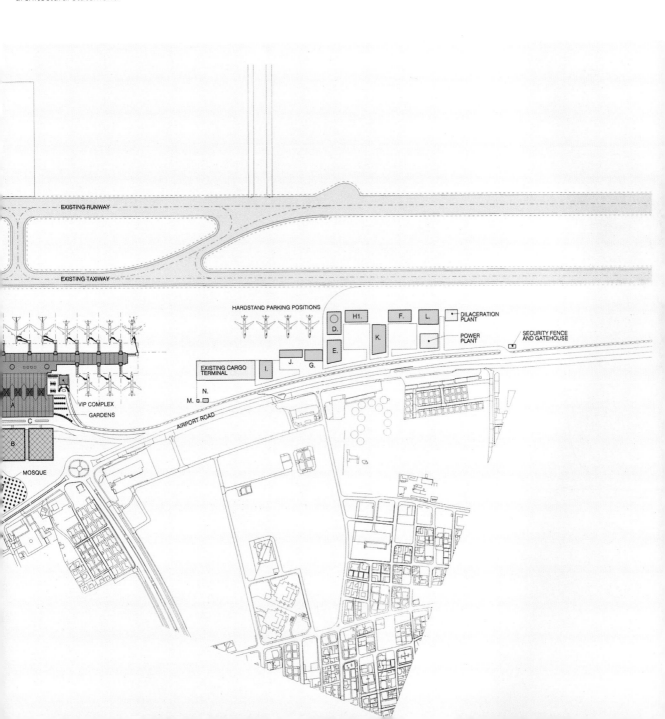

*Below left:* Control tower
*Below right:* Fire Station
*Facing page top:* Old merchant house
*Facing page bottom:* Control tower

40

### Component I
### Support Buildings

Due to imminent needs for increased capacity, the project began with upgrades to the existing airport and the creation of new facilities, including a control tower, fire station, and aircraft support facilities. Many of these facilities were beyond repair, and were simply replaced. The new site for these facilities, called the Center Zone, was located equidistant from the north and south ends of the taxi and runway system. All of the upgraded and new facilities were designed with the winning design in mind. They drew inspiration from the forts that line the city and coast, as well as from local patterns and the signature white color of the Doha's built environment.

*Below:* Fishermen on a dhow
*Bottom:* Curbside
*Facing page:* Ticketing hall

## Component II
## Passenger Terminal Complex

Fentress Bradburn was awarded first place in the 1996 international design competition for DOH with a design based on the preliminary master plan. The parameters for this plan were governed by the Ministry's limited financial resources, modest growth in air traffic volume, and an uncertain future over hubbing operations. However, in two short years strong economic growth and positive changes in the local airline industry led to significant increases in available funding, and, consequently, a total revision of the master plan and passenger terminal program.

After several iterations, the final plan for Component II resolved to increase the terminal complex's footprint and relocate the entire facility to a Greenfield site immediately adjacent to the existing airport complex. While changes occurred to the project's scope, including the number of gates and the addition of vehicular access roads, the complex's design remained constant: a structure representative of a traditional Qatari *dhow*, or wooden fishing ship. With curving low masts and triangular *lateen*-rigged sails, the ship's form is one of tradition, drama, and motion.

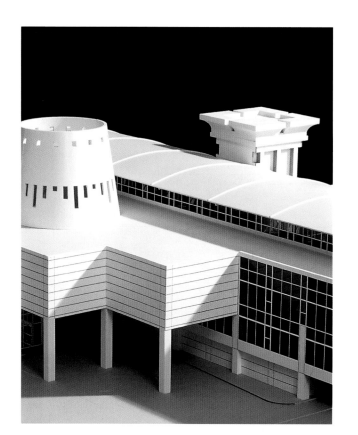

44

The ticketing hall roof springs from central supporting masts that rise like the underbelly of a ship. Structural beams tie together panes of glass, recalling the primary joints of these wooden sailing vessels. The same sense of place is carried through security, where an inverted replica of the curbside design curves a quarter circle overhead and is carried along the full length of the concourse. Lounges for the 20 attached jetbridges are carpeted and cloistered, bringing a sense of rhythm and calm to the often harried passengers. Interspersed among the lounges are retail hubs designed to mimic fortress turrets. These double-height spaces are common areas for food courts and retail outlets.

Richly detailed patterns used on floors, walls, and exterior glass are influenced by traditional Qatari textile patterns. Finely detailed frit patterns for the skylights and curtainwalls were inspired by the Qatar National Museum, formally home to Sheikh Abdullah Al Thani. Cast-in-place and precast white and sand-colored concrete complete the exterior palette, recalling Qatari architectural coloration and the sands of Qatar's great inland sea.

## Component III
### Control Tower

Ensuring the safety of passengers and aircraft was the most critical planning objective in the overall development of DOH. The site selected for the ATCT afforded the best line of sight to aircrafts as they moved throughout the airfield. Additionally, the design of the tower was considered critical, given its prominent location and high visibility. The tower is the first image arriving passengers see, whether by land or air, and therefore it is symbolic of the airport and region.

The tower's design was informed by the color, massing, and materials of the passenger terminal. In elevation, it was also inspired by native palm trees; decorative hash marks recall the trunk of the palm, while green glass clad around the control space mimics the tree's regal leaves.

*Page 44 top:* Model depicting retail turret along concourse
*Page 44 bottom:* Concourse lined with retail
*Page 45:* Cross section of retail turret with skylight
*Above:* Palm tree backlit by a sunset
*Right:* ATCT with renovated terminal

# JCN

Terminal & Concourse
Incheon International Airport

| | |
|---|---|
| location | Incheon Bay, Seoul, South Korea |
| conditions | new construction, Greenfield site |
| type | multi-airline hub, O&D |
| area | 5,935,000 sqft (550,000 sqm) |
| annual pax | 50 million at capacity<br>*UD: 100 million* |
| gates | 46 attached<br>*UD: 174* |
| scope | programming, planning, design,<br>& construction |

### Background

Gimpo International Airport, JCN's predecessor and what has become the domestic airport of Seoul, struggled to handle Seoul's growing air traffic during the late 1980s and throughout the 1990s. With international passenger and cargo numbers rising beyond the capacity of Gimpo, operators and political officials sought to create a new, mindfully master planned airport that would showcase the depth and breadth of Korean culture and the country's role as a leader in Asia.

An international design jury was assembled to decide on a pool of competitors and ultimately select the winning team. Fentress Bradburn Architects—in association with a consortium of four Korean architectural firms called KACI—won this competition. The jury felt that their design "fully understands [that] this new world-class hub airport will be the gateway to Korea of the new age. Its efforts to draw harmony between Korean images and global design trends and technologies are outstanding."

JCN is situated on a man-made land bridge connecting two islands, 18.5 miles (30 kilometers) from Seoul, just off the coast of Incheon City. Incheon Bay first became known to millions as the site on which General Douglas MacArthur's amphibious landings ultimately turned the tide of the Korean War in 1950. Since its 2001 opening, over 150 million passengers and 10,000 employees have come to know it as the new home of JCN. Continuously ranked as one of the world's top airports, JCN is an exemplary patron of the human experience.

In 2004, the airport's 38 million passengers were served by 44 boarding gates, 18 hard stands, and two runways. By 2020, that number of passengers is expected to more than double to 79 million. By then, the airport will have completed the full build-out of its ultimate development by adding an additional landside terminal, two more runways, 130 new gates on four remote linear concourses that connect to the existing terminal by an underground APM, and all the requisite support buildings.

### Master Plan

Like Brasilia, the capitol city of Brazil, Incheon's business district was intentionally master planned to maximize efficiency, promote a singular contextually based identity, and meet the needs of the core industry—herein, aviation. This district, also known as an "aerotropolis" or "winged city," will host many of the facilities that are still in the planning or construction phases. Ultimate development will feature exhibition halls, hotels, office buildings, apartment complexes, retail outlets, restaurants, and sports stadia.

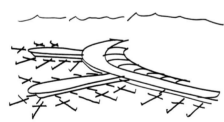

Between 2005, when Incheon International Airport Corporation (IIAC) opens a double-track railway to Gimpo, and 2007, when direct high-speed rail service extends from Seoul, the area surrounding JCN will continue to become more urban. In the meantime, people make their way to JCN via a dedicated, amply wide expressway in public buses, personal cars, car services, and other chartered vehicles.

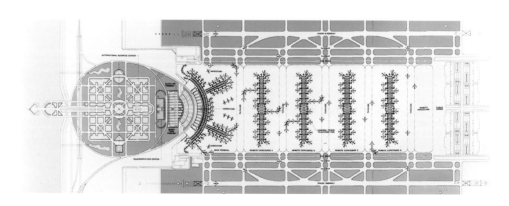

**Landside Departure Experience**

The curved form of the terminal embraces passengers. Curbside canopies reach out beyond the canted curtainwall to offer shelter from the elements, while steel grids swoop and fly overhead with high-tech exuberance. The vaulted roof of the terminal itself sits on long-spanning tubular steel compression trusses. Vertically straight and horizontally curving elements recall early Korean Palaces and reflect the area's marine context. In addition to its aesthetic aspects, the unique roof structure capitalizes on local materials, in this case, steel. Korea's steel industry is one of the largest and most technically sophisticated in the world.

**Ticketing**

At JCN, the 250 check-in counters are islands, laid out in modular units, surrounded by e-ticketing kiosks. Departing passengers flow around them in fluid circulation patterns. Once checked in, passengers continue on to the concourse level where they enter either one of 28 security checkpoint stations or a passport control and customs declaration area.

*Above:* Seoul and the Namdaemun
*Right:* Sketch by Curtis Worth Fentress
*Bottom:* Check-in counters inside the ticketing hall
*Facing page:* Bridges from the curbside into the ticketing hall

52

## Great Courtyard

JCN combines tectonics with cultural warmth and symbolism, a mix at home in modern Korea. Carved into the core of the symmetrical terminal is the Great Courtyard, which serves to organize the facility by addressing pedestrian traffic-flow patterns. Glass elevators connect and activate all five levels of the airport, including transportation facilities, concessions, and airport handling operations. Interior landmarks help people orient themselves, and therefore easily find their way through the terminal. Each element of the courtyard was meticulously planned and engineered. Art, banners, color, and landscape distinguish intersections and highlight destinations. Passengers, visitors, and employees alike pass through this memorable space.

## Materials

Another local material, Korean granite, wraps three sides of the security area, serving to enclose sensitive spaces, while symbolically referencing the traditional stone gates of the city of Seoul. Wood paneling and soothing colors, designed to lower stress levels, line the walls of the security and customs areas. After passing through them, departing passengers emerge into the bright expanse of the concourse itself.

*Facing page top:* Great Hall connecting all five active levels of the terminal
*Facing page bottom left:* Monk in the inner courtyard of Bulguksa Temple
*Facing page bottom right:* Playground in Busan, South Korea
*Right:* Rendering of Great Hall
*Below:* Section from curbside to airside

## Concessions

A wide variety of retail, food, and beverage offerings are strategically placed throughout the terminal. While the highest concentration of these amenities is within the multi-level, central Great Courtyard, additional concessions occur at passenger flow intersections: along concourse passageways, in the boarding lounges, and in the international arrivals hall. With over 44 duty-free shops and over 150 concessions, JCN caters to the needs of passengers, visitors, and employees alike. While consumers benefit from the added convenience, IIAC benefits from high levels of non-airline generated revenue.

55

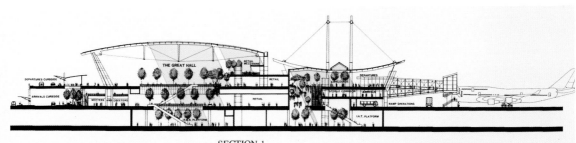

SECTION 1

*Left:* Skylights in terminal
*Below left:* Detail drawing of jet bridge
*Below right:* Glass-walled permanent jet bridge

## Skylights, Curtainwalls, and Clerestories

Skylights, glass curtainwalls, and clerestories not only save energy by bathing the space in natural light, they also reinforce the building's already intuitive passenger flows. In the ticketing hall, they start at each curbside entry portal and continue above the circulation path between ticket islands to the security checkpoints. Along the concourse, a central spine of skylights reinforces the circulation routes to gates and concessions.

While 55 skylights and their nearby clerestories are interspersed throughout the passenger terminal and its attached concourses, the majority of light enters through floor-to-ceiling glass curtainwalls that line the concourses and flank the terminal. The terminal's two 12,100-square-foot (1,125-square-meter) curtainwalls supply a dramatic backdrop for ticketing, passenger holding, and duty-free shopping. Additional light envelops arriving and departing passengers as they venture through the 46 apron-drive, glass passenger boarding bridges.

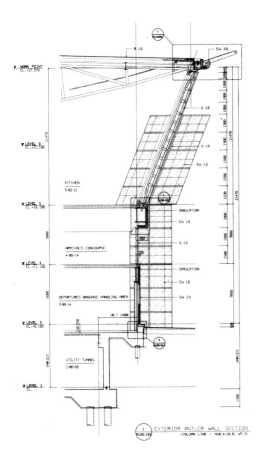

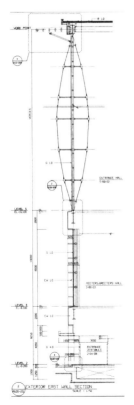

60

### Airside

Arriving aircraft, including the new A380 and Boeing 777, land on either of two runways, which are spaced to accommodate simultaneous takeoffs. Once on the ground, international arrival passengers unload through dual passenger bridges. To further expedite this arrivals process, inspection facilities feature 120 immigration and 50 customs counters.

Advanced flight information systems receive radar information from arriving aircraft that is then transmitted to baggage handling facilities, gate management systems, and public address displays. This technology was first employed at JCN and has since been utilized by several other airports. A redundant system stands ready to operate in the event that any or all of the functions need to be operated manually.

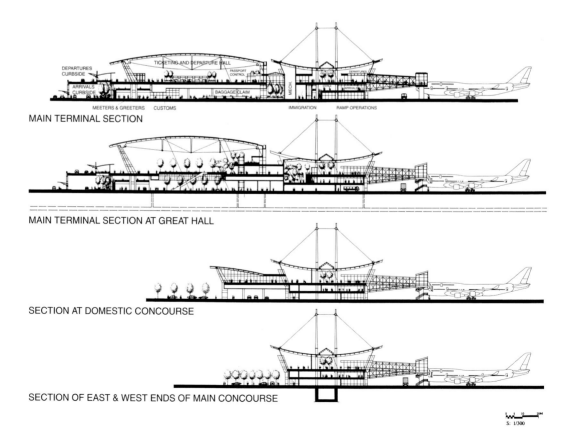

MAIN TERMINAL SECTION

MAIN TERMINAL SECTION AT GREAT HALL

SECTION AT DOMESTIC CONCOURSE

SECTION OF EAST & WEST ENDS OF MAIN CONCOURSE

S: 1/300

## Concourse

A system of moving sidewalks minimizes walking distances to less than 400 feet (120 meters) from curbside to gate. Departing and transferring passengers with time on their hands can make use of a convenient and fully equipped business center. For even longer stays, there is a small city of services and restaurants on the mezzanine level.

After taking advantage of the concessions and other opportunities in the concourse and boarding lounges, passengers enter permanent glass bridges that take them out to the glass jetway and onto the aircraft. This moment of visual connection with parked and taxiing jets stands in sharp contrast to the ubiquitous dark tunnel to and from the aircraft portals at other airports. At JCN, the glass bridge occurs at all of the 46 gates outfitted to service type D, E, and new generation aircraft. The curve of the concourse serves as the best geometry for aircraft push-back operations and for the formulation of a building module based on the wing span of type D aircraft. This combination of curves and modules allows for easy expansion capabilities as traffic continues to grow.

### Landside Arrivals Experience

Arrival at JCN is literally staged, with passengers entering the airport on a translucent mezzanine from which they descend to the meeters-and-greeters areas and baggage claim. An exception to the typical airport plan, baggage claim is a tall, bright, open space, clearly visible from several vantage points.

Meeters and greeters waiting in the international arrivals hall don't have to wait long to meet arriving passengers with checked baggage thanks to the high-speed baggage handling system. JCN's baggage system handles each bag within five minutes from input into the system and can process up 32,000 items hourly. Eight slope plate baggage claim carousels disperse luggage to awaiting passengers.

### Sustainability

JCN propelled sustainable design in airports to a new level. Dredging methods and the design of the drainage system, silt pond, and water-tight barrier ensure environmental protection. Airport waste products are collected and separated for recycling. Inflammable wastes are saved and incinerated as an energy source. Ninety percent of the water used daily is recycled and used to clean the airport's buildings. The self-sufficient airport is landscaped with 40,000 trees native to the island, plus 600,000 flowering trees. Meanwhile, the terminal's interior features are landscaped with 60-foot-tall (20-meter-tall) Korean Pine trees. Penetration of daylight into the passenger terminal interior through clerestories increases the structure's energy efficiency.

Impact data on the noise level, the oceanic ecosystem, and air pollution levels continue to be constantly collected and analyzed to ensure high levels of sustainability.

*Page 62:* Concourse roof trusses over skylights
*Page 63 top:* Moving sidewalks span the full length of the concourse
*Page 63 bottom left:* Colonnaded Walk at Bulguksa Temple
*Page 63 bottom right:* Gate lounges
*Facing page top left:* Arrivals curbside lined with landscaping outside baggage claim level
*Facing page top right:* Meeters and greeters hall
*Facing page bottom:* Concourse and jet bridges

# TFS

Terminal & Concourses
Reina Sofia International Airport

| | |
|---|---|
| location | Tenerife-Sur, Canary Islands, Spain |
| condition | new construction, Brownfield site |
| type | O&D |
| area | 250,000 sqft (23,200 sqm)<br>*UD: 1,000,000 sqft (92,900 sqm)* |
| annual pax | 20 million at capacity<br>*UD: 75 million* |
| gates | 24 attached & detached<br>*UD: 158* |
| scope | design competition entry |

Previous page: Section model from people mover to curbside
*Below left:* Anaga Cliffs along Tenerife's coastline
*Below right:* "Isis Holistic Center" set amid volcanic debris
*Right:* Site plans from Phase I through ultimate development

68

## Master Plan

Located in the Atlantic Ocean, among the Canary Islands and just off the coast of Africa, Tenerife-Sur is a tourist hotspot for Europeans and acts as an economic engine for its Spanish authority. Even with expansions, the existing airport terminal was struggling to keep pace with its annual passenger traffic growth, which was expected to reach 1,200 passengers at peak periods. Airport officials also aimed to improve the experience of departing passengers who often spent several hours in the terminal between hotel check-out and flight departure times. They wanted to create a comfortable, resort-like facility that extended the traveler's vacation experience.

The master plan solution accommodates five phases of development—from a single terminal with one remote, two-finger concourse, to two terminals with three remote, four-finger concourses. In addition to incremental, need-based expansion, this phasing scenario also allows seamless, continuous operations during construction.

## Site Issues

Located on the southwestern side of the island, embedded on a hillside of volcanic rock, the new airport complex's topography was to be one of the most challenging aspects of its design and planning, largely due to grade change from one side of the apron to the other.

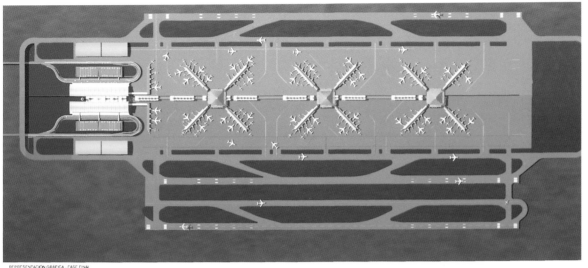

REPRESENTACIÓN GRÁFICA - FASE FINAL
RENDERED SITE PLAN

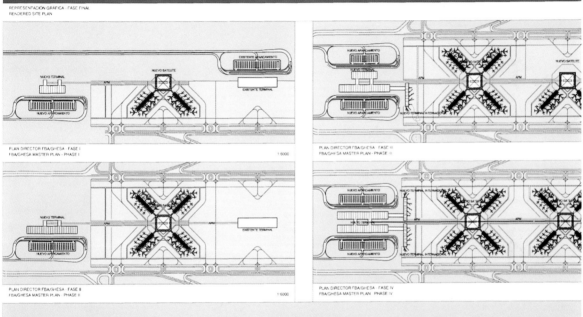

PLAN DIRECTOR FBA/GHESA - FASE I
FBA/GHESA MASTER PLAN - PHASE I                    1:6000

PLAN DIRECTOR FBA/GHESA - FASE III
FBA/GHESA MASTER PLAN - PHASE III

PLAN DIRECTOR FBA/GHESA - FASE II
FBA/GHESA MASTER PLAN - PHASE II                   1:6000

PLAN DIRECTOR FBA/GHESA - FASE IV
FBA/GHESA MASTER PLAN - PHASE IV

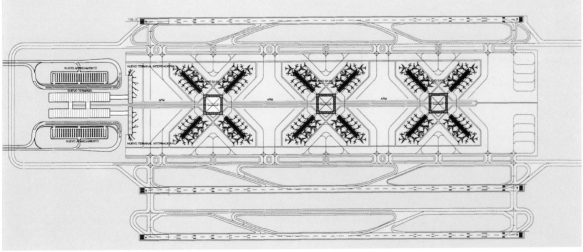

Below left: Windsurfer in El Medano
Below right: Bathers at Arena Beach
Facing page top: Aerial computer rendering of ultimate development
Facing page bottom: Peaked sails rise above the terminal's people mover station

70

**Landside Experience**

Whether arriving or departing, passengers journeying through Tenerife-Sur begin or retain all that a holiday experience in Tenerife-Sur entails. The clean lines of the sailing vessels that frequent the island can be seen in the rooflines of the curbside drop-off canopies and the open-air structure that covers the at-grade APM. Inside the enclosed ticketing hall, minimal three-dimensional trusses above a curtainwall structure establish transparency and bring the outdoors inside. Live palm trees on the interior further express continuity with the region's beautiful outdoors and reinforce the airport's tropical environment.

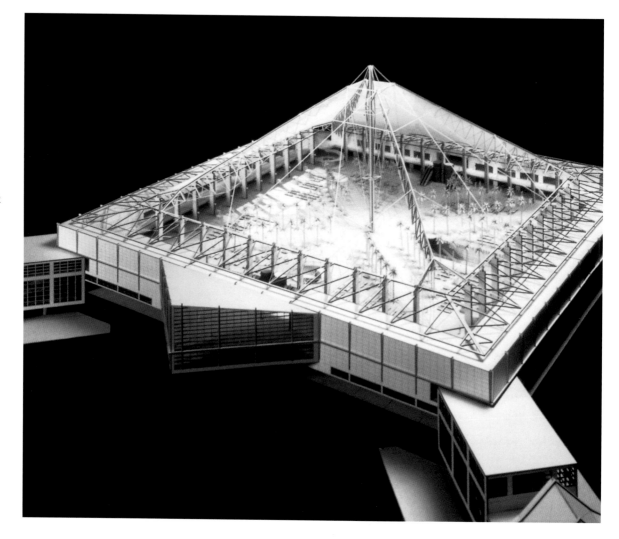

*Facing page top:* Model of Central Plaza, the nexus of each concourse
*Facing page bottom:* Section of Central Plaza with train station on left
*Below left:* Palm-lined parkway in front of Hotel Mencey
*Below right:* Timeshare resort

## Airside Experience

An intentional emphasis was placed on programming the interiors of the Central Plazas at each of the four satellite concourses. In each plaza, four three-dimensional trusses form a pyramid to support the fabric roof. This roof, hovering above the upper walls of the plaza, introduces natural ventilation and acts as one more component in maintaining a connection with the sultry paradise just outside.

Square at their bases, these plazas serve as the hub for up to four pier concourses that extend from each corner. Floor patterns are reminiscent of local foliage with peaked petals that aid circulation flow. Nestled among the palm trees, the lounge area in each plaza affords a respite for passengers with extended layovers.

## Concessions

Operating as the nexus of the facility, where passengers arrive and depart by means of an APM, the Central Plaza satellites contain a wide variety of local and branded concessions. Retail, food, and beverage services line the central courtyard from which pier concourses radiate. These open spaces aid in passenger orientation and circulation.

# SEA

Central Terminal Redevelopment
Seattle-Tacoma International Airport

| | |
|---|---|
| location | Seattle, Washington, USA |
| condition | renovation, reuse & expansion, Brownfield site |
| type | multi-airline hub, O&D |
| area | 390,000 sqft (22,300 sqm) |
| annual pax | 45 million at capacity |
| retail | up to 30 outlets 41,500 sqft (3,850 sqm) |
| scope | programming, planning, design, & construction |

### Background

Seismic reinforcement served as the primary catalyst for redeveloping the central terminal. The 1949 administration building was the original passenger terminal and is one of the oldest structures at SEA. Given the project's necessity and scope, airport operators decided to maximize this opportunity. In addition to enhancing the facility's life safety program, they placed a concerted emphasis on improving the overall passenger experience.

The Port of Seattle set out with a definitive and inspiring vision: to restore excitement for travel, provide comforts and conveniences to a diverse audience, be an expression of the Pacific Northwest region, and operate as the central heart of the entire complex. Upon opening, over 30 million passengers experience the manifestation of these visions and more.

### Phasing

Phasing and construction sequencing were the most challenging aspects of the project. The central terminal is located at the intersection of four concourses and adjacent to the aircraft parking area operated by Delta and the airport's busiest airline, Horizon. The project had to maintain seamless airport operations during the relocation of airfield utilities, excavation of a basement, alternation of baggage and tug routes through construction areas, relocation and consolidation of security checkpoints, and terminal modifications from ticketing to boarding gates.

### Infrastructure

In addition to the central terminal expansion and redevelopment, the Port of Seattle also requested the expansion and renovation of Horizon Airlines' facilities. A new outbound baggage area was created for their system under the newly expanded central terminal, bringing it closer to the airline's ramp operations. Horizon's operation from new hold rooms on Concourses B and C now permits better access to ground-loaded aircraft. The existing ramp level and ground-loaded, commuter aircraft parking positions were also relocated to provide an additional 18 positions.

### Seismic Upgrades

Since the 6.8-magnitude Nisqually Earthquake in February 2001 that caused $4 million worth of damage to the airport's control tower, seismic code upgrades have become an intricate component of all the airport's projects. Upgrades to the terminal were coordinated with upgrades to the concourses, control tower, and administration building because of their interdependency. The expanded terminal buttresses the administration building, and new concrete sheer walls and steel bracing were integrated into both the terminal's existing structure and its new construction.

**76**

*Previous page:*
Central terminal from mid-airfield

*Below:*
Site plan, central terminal highlighted with hash marks

*Facing page top:*
Historic photo of entry to original 1949 terminal

*Facing page bottom:*
Artists rendering of section depicting project scope

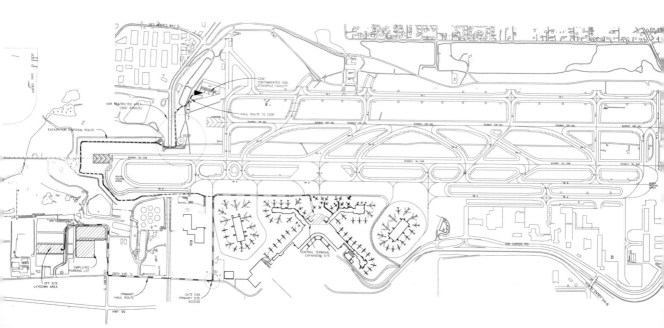

*Right:*
Early massing and
study model

*Below right:*
Early massing and
study model

*Facing page:*
Dawn view of
curtainwall with
a 777 tail in
foreground

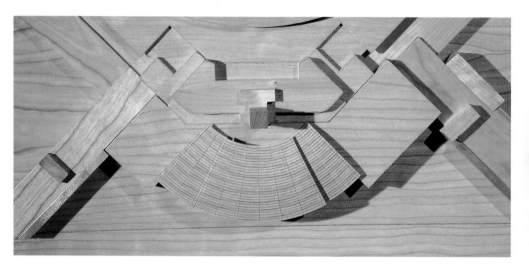

## Concept

Observation decks were a major feature of the original central terminal, which opened in 1949. From these observation decks, passengers and their companions could watch landings and takeoffs, as well as take in the area's natural beauty. In the Pacific Northwest region of the United States where the cities of Seattle and Tacoma lie, mountains, forests, and ocean come together in a dramatic way that is often captured in pictures of Mount Rainier. Air travelers were denied the pleasure of these scenes when, in 1962, renovations eliminated the views altogether.

Left: Pacific Marketplace
Below right: Detail of bi-directionally-curved curtainwall

## Curtainwall

The 250,000-square-foot (23,225-square-meter) expansion began with a desire to resurrect observation capabilities in a way that honored both the building's Art Deco heritage and modern day technological achievements. Massing models were some of the first means used to explore options, particularly given that the site dictated eastward expansion into the tarmac. Creating a fan-shaped indoor civic marketplace, as opposed to elongating the historical trapezoid, was the chosen solution. The fan shape actually occurs both in plan and elevation; its two form givers, the roof and curtainwall, respectively honor Art Deco and technological advancement.

As passengers enter from the low-ceilinged security checkpoint, the ceiling steps up dramatically from the original structure and arcs, revealing the expansion. Dropped wings, connected via clerestories that span over retail outlets, flank the elegant primary ceiling form. Contrasting with these historical forms is a unique and innovative curtainwall. Bi-directionally curved, it is the largest of its kind in North America. While its 60 feet (18 meters) in height are vertically convex, its 350 feet (106 meters) in length are horizontally concave. The curtainwall is a captivating lens that is in itself an engineering feat, much like the aircraft it showcases. For passengers, the continuity between the two elements comes in their sinuous shapes.

## Pacific Marketplace

The space formed by these symbolic and sinuous shapes evokes the feel of the recently rehabilitated Union Station in Seattle and Grand Central Station in New York. However, instead of being similarly vacuous, the great indoor civic plaza, also known as the Pacific Marketplace, is filled with seating and landscaping to establish a welcome respite for the leisure, connecting, or harried traveler. Images of Pioneer Square, Tacoma Park, and Pike Place Market come to mind when viewing this space, as do Frank Lloyd Wright's words, "Buildings are made for life to be lived in happily."

As the airport's new "crowning jewel"—a term first used by former director, Gina Marie Lindsey—the 130,000-square-foot (12,000-square-meter) Pacific Marketplace succeeds because of a combination of strategic elements: an extremely efficient layout, over 40,000 square feet (3,700 square meters) of concessions, and four giant FIDs that are easily viewable from anywhere within the 500-seat indoor marketplace. It is a place conducive for friends, family, business associates, and individuals to shop, eat, or simply relax with daylight and dramatic views.

*Right:*
FIDs above centralized security checkpoint

*Facing page:*
Pacific Marketplace with *Landing,* by Helmick and Schechter

84

### Retail Esplanades

Post-security circulation begins at the core of
the Pacific Marketplace so that passengers may
make use of any number of its amenities before
journeying down either of the shop-lined "streets."
These streets branch left and right to efficiently
direct passengers to gates on concourse A, B, C, or
D, and to APMs that service the north and south
satellites.

The central section of the streets was remodeled
to provide spacious circulation as well as maintain
an architecturally consistent look and feel. Retail
services and merchandising kiosks, previously
located in the center of the building, were relocated
to the east wall in order to create the feeling of an
extended avenue.

## Security

Passengers are routed into the Pacific Marketplace via a consolidated central security checkpoint, which has the expansion capacity to nearly double. The conscious decision to replace and consolidate security from the previous two checkpoints was three-fold. It cuts down on the likelihood of a breach, because the same staff are responsible for only a single area. It also enhances TSA's ability to open additional positions during peak periods. And it aids in post-security circulation by congregating passengers to a single point from which clear signage directs them on to their intermediate and final destinations.

## Details

The dominant themes of the Pacific Northwest and Art Deco are also played out in the details. Custom light fixtures take the form of outdoor lampposts with seasonal plantings. Exterior-style metal railings define seating areas, while varied storefronts, surrounded by hanging plants, help create the image of a downtown scene from Seattle or Tacoma. Public elevator doors are engraved with a custom wing design found on glass elements from the old security pavilion. A terrazzo floor pattern, utilizing the design of a compass from the original 1949 building documents, marks the entrance to the consolidated security checkpoint. And a custom dolphin frieze recalling the terracotta molds found above the passenger elevator doors adorns the façade of the renovated 1949 administration building.

*Left:* Centralized security checkpoint pre-Pacific Marketplace
*Below:* Dolphin frieze borders the historic façade
*Below right:* Seasonal flower baskets hang from streetlight lampposts

# MUC

Terminal 2
Munich International Airport

| | |
|---|---|
| location | Munich, Germany |
| condition | new construction, Brownfield site |
| type | single-airline hub, O&D |
| area | 2,150,000 sqft (198,500) sqm |
| annual pax | 25 million at capacity |
| gates | 106 |
| scope | design competition entry |

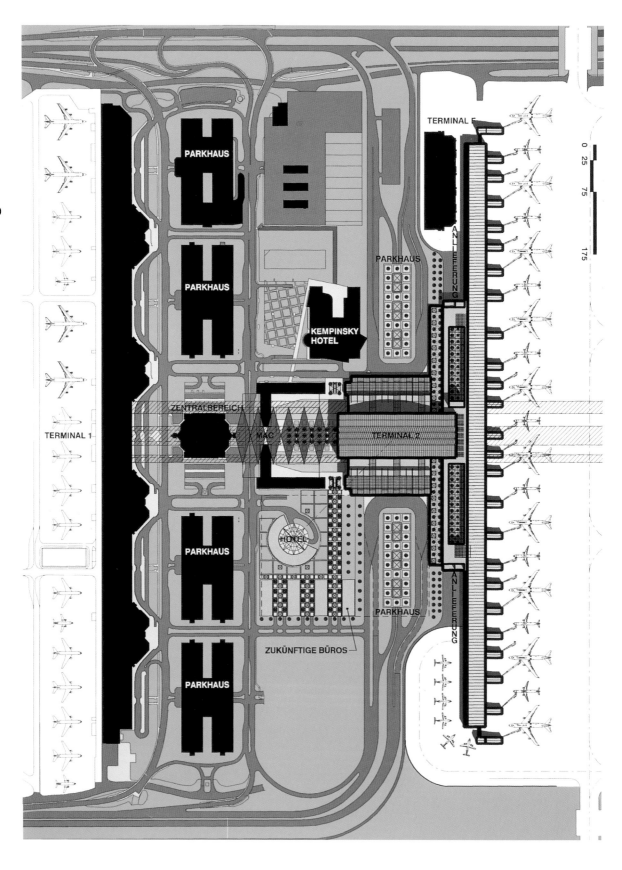

## Master Plan

The program for MUC's Terminal 2 (T2) called for all the facilities necessary to independently accommodate hubbing operations, including: a new landside terminal facility, domestic and international concourses, structured parking, and requisite elevated and at-grade roadways. Provisions were also to be made for a future hotel and office complex. MUC officials envisioned a sustainable design solution that would be in architectural harmony with the existing Munich Airport Center (MAC) and Terminal 1 (T1), maintain established circulation flows, and provide the highest level of passenger comfort and convenience—all within a transparent, voluminous, and open structure.

Architectural harmony between T2 and the existing airport facilities, namely MAC and T1, was established in several ways. A detached roofline was designed to be a statement unto itself—a complementary structure that further defines the airport's overall campus while preparing the facility for future additions. The massing of T2 was derived from MAC to create a visual connection between the two buildings, which are physically connected on levels two, three, and four. The S-bahn station on level two forms a direct, enclosed connection between T1 and T2. The landscaping on level three helps to create a literal connection between the MAC Forum and T2. And on level four, MAC's exterior walkways link with T2 to both physically and visually connect the two facilities.

The terminal design consists of three modules: the south, central, and north. Simple, logical phasing scenarios are designed to maintain flexible operations for T2. Even though the full structure of the landside terminal would be built as part of Phase I, the north terminal module and its curbsides would remain a shell. Baggage claim facilities not required in Phase I could be utilized as temporary office spaces until expansion occurs. When necessary, the center module could be constructed along with the Great Square and south landside module. Similarly, the south and north concourse modules could be added as needs require.

The design for T2 is economical both in construction and in long-term operating costs. A repetitive 33- by 33-foot (ten- by ten-meter) grid composes the uniquely designed structural roof system of both the terminal and the concourse. This repetitive and simple approach not only makes the roof less expensive to procure, it also makes it easier to construct.

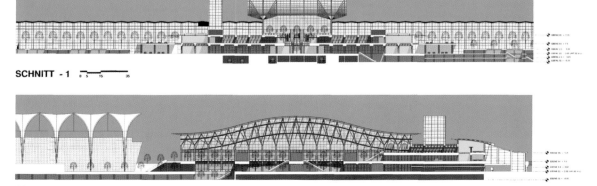

**SCHNITT - 1**

**SCHNITT - 2**

## Landside Departure Experience

Passengers arriving to T2 in personal vehicles park in a garage that flanks the landside terminal directly adjacent to the departures and arrivals curbsides. Seven levels of parking comprise the garage: four below-grade, one at-grade level, and two above-grade. Locating the majority of parking below grade not only minimizes the parking structure's visual impact, it also helps maintain view corridors beyond the airport's immediate context.

Once at curbside, passengers are greeted by generously dimensioned forecourt gardens that highlight local flora and fauna. The interior courtyards feature much of the same foliage and help maintain an outdoor feeling throughout T2.

## Ticketing Hall

Departing passengers are greeted and oriented inside a spacious ticketing hall that segues into security screening, outbound customs and immigration facilities, concessions, and more. Inside ticketing, the interplay between light and shadow can be controlled by mechanical louvers that protect horizontal glazing. Curtainwalls, clerestories, and interior glass walls screen any glare with the help of overhangs, while washing nearly all of the interior spaces with soft, natural light.

*Page 88:* Curbside approach
*Page 90:* Ultimate development master plan
*Page 91 top:* Existing architecture, Terminal C
*Page 91 bottom:* Elevations
*Below:* Aerial on axis with curbside drop-off roadway
*Facing page top:* Rooftop garden
*Facing page bottom:* Hall of Antiquities at Munich Residenz

*Left:* The Viktualienmarkt, the main food market in Munich
*Facing page bottom:* Great Square
*Below:* Escalators deliver passengers to lower level baggage claim

## Great Square

A central Great Square organizes the terminal portion of the facility and offers passengers a unique and interesting spatial experience. A sense of transparency and spaciousness is achieved through the systematic arrangement of ceiling apertures and glass façades. These also establish a relationship between the exterior and interior, creating a bright and friendly environment. The result is a simple, easily understood airport terminal that focuses on the needs of its passengers.

## Landscaping

Along with daylighting, extensive garden areas are designed to soften the hard edges of the building and reduce its perceived mass. Forecourts at curbside and interior courtyards provide a clear separation between landside and airside. Gardens are featured in both public areas and office spaces to bring all users of the facility in touch with nature.

### Concessions

Convenient placement of concessions encourages passengers to take advantage of the facility's numerous and diverse services. Concessions line the departure experience from ticket counters through to gate lounges, while arrivals passengers access concessions along the concourses, all the way to the curbsides.

### Airside Arrival Experience

International and domestic arrivals pass through spacious boarding lounges on the way to bus gates, outbound passport control areas, the Great Hall, and baggage claim. All of the lounges are washed in natural light, helping acclimate jet-lagged passengers, while creating a comfortable space that connects passengers with nature.

*Below:* Existing concourse
*Bottom:* Section through Great Square
*Facing page top:* Departure level floor plan at ultimate development
*Facing page bottom:* Aerial with concourse in foreground

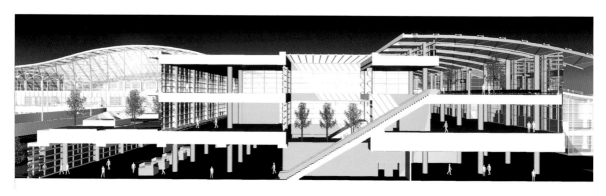

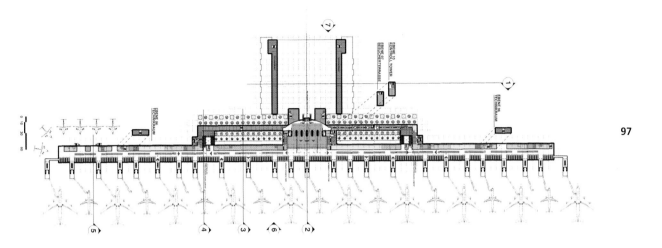

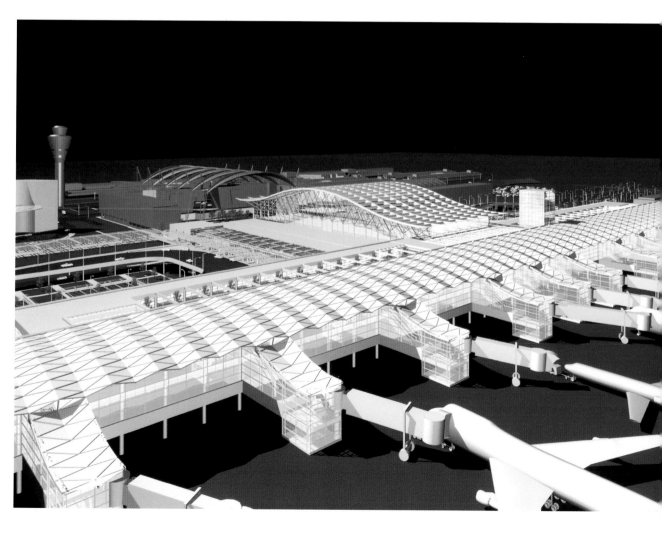

# RDU

Terminal C & Concourse Redevelopment
Raleigh-Durham International Airport

| | |
|---|---|
| location | Raleigh, North Carolina, USA |
| condition | new construction, Brownfield site |
| type | multi-airline hub, O&D |
| area | 765,000 sqft (79,000 sqm) *UD: 1,000,000 sqft (92,900 sqm)* |
| annual pax | 35 million at capacity *UD: 50 million* |
| gates | 31 attached & detached *UD: 44* |
| scope | planning, design, & construction |

## Master Plan

In the mid 1990s, a growing number of airlines constricted operations at Terminal A, which was reaching capacity at peak travel times. At the same time, Terminal C was operating within capacity, but as an American Airlines–owned hub. So in 2002, when American Airlines decided to completely relinquish their ownership of Terminal C, RDU officials made the decision to acquire it.

With two terminals under their purview, RDU considered their options for redevelopment and expansion. Since Terminal C was underutilized and not conducive to O&D operations—it only offered half the ticketing, security, and baggage claim stations because it had been a hub—airport officials decided to focus their attention on redeveloping Terminal C first.

As officials collaborated with the design team, they kept at the forefront of the planning efforts RDU's vision statement: "To be the best airport in the world, known for its uncompromising service as judged by customers, employees, and owners."

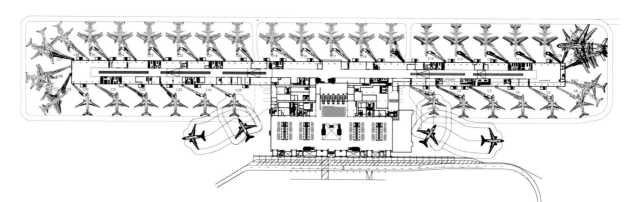

The end result is a two-story landside terminal building, with an attached, Boeing 777-friendly airside concourse that has a sterile corridor to accommodate international flights.

## Phasing

A four-phase plan to redevelop Terminal C resulted from prudent planning and programming by the design team, in conjunction with the RDU Airport Authority and its board members. All phases were designed to accommodate continuous operations of the airport throughout construction.

The first phase, completed in Spring 2005, involved partial demolition of the landside terminal building and the north end of the airside concourse to prepare for the next phase. Phase II, set to open in 2008, involves constructing approximately half of the landside terminal, which will comprise two ticketing islands, three baggage claim carousels, the security checkpoint, a new international arrivals facility, and a portion of the Great Hall. The new 17-gate north concourse will also be completed in Phase II. Upon completion of Phase II, Phase III will commence. During this phase, the remaining portion of the original landside terminal and portions of the remaining concourse will be demolished; building of the next segment of the landside terminal will begin and will comprise one ticketing island, two baggage carousels, the remainder of the central portal, and an additional 120 feet (37 meters) of new concourse with one additional gate.

The final phase, also referred to as "Ultimate Development," includes constructing the final segment of the landside terminal, demolishing the existing south concourse, and constructing a new expanded south concourse.

*Previous page:* Departure curbside
*Left:* Site plan at ultimate development
*Below:* Aerial of ultimate development

*Right:*
Rural road in autumn

*Below:*
Great Smoky
Mountains National
Park

*Facing page top:*
Pedestrian bridge
canopy leading to
ticketing hall

*Facing page bottom:*
Signature entry to
ticketing hall

## Landside Departure Experience

Terminal C is a memorable gateway; it is a timeless expression of Raleigh-Durham's regional culture. As a civic space, the terminal succeeds by being easy to navigate, highly flexible, and iconic. The major exterior and interior architectural elements are abstractions of North Carolina's agricultural, textile, and hi-tech communities.

Departing passengers who parked in the adjacent parking facility reach the departure and ticketing area on the facility's upper level, by traversing a 30-foot-wide (nine-meter-wide) pedestrian bridge sheltered by a glass and steel canopy. This canopy is the leading element in a series of hills that comprise the roof of both the terminal and concourse. The rolling roof recalls the natural landscape of the Piedmont region, while curbside canopies evoke images of textile machines, representative of an industry that has long sustained much of the local economy. The curbside canopies and roof forms also reinforce the architectural vernacular of canopies that occur at parking pay booths and an observation stand near the Airport's General Aviation Terminal.

104

### Ticketing

The ticketing hall is at once welcoming and informative. Each of the four ticketing islands accommodates up to 20 stations. Ample spacing between and around the islands is designed to accommodate the placement of e-ticketing machines and their potential reconfiguration. In fact, the space is column-free, and baggage drops are centrally located to accommodate any future changes that become necessary in the passenger check-in area.

Wooden lenticular roof trusses give the space a sense of scale and rhythm and also represent the local wooded countryside and its rich heritage of carpentry and crafts. Carpet patterns are inspired by local quilts and DNA sequences, which recall the biomedical component of the region's Research Triangle. In high traffic areas, richly-toned terrazzo flooring provides a durable walking surface that complements both the carpet and roof trusses.

Warm natural light washes over interior finishes as it enters through ample vertical glazing and clerestories. The clerestories are placed between the undulating trusses and corrugated ceiling segments, which rise between ticketing islands and above the Central Atrium. This atrium connects to baggage claim, bringing daylight well into the lower level.

## Daylighting

Extensive curtainwalls throughout Terminal C showcase North Carolina's lush vegetation to connect travelers with their immediate surroundings, and increase the excitement for travel as passengers witness airplanes on the runways and tarmac. The curtainwalls also invite a healthy amount of sunshine to wash both levels of the interior, on the landside and on the entire length of the airside concourse.

Clear-vision glass transitions to partially fritted–vision glass along the upper portions of the exterior walls. The fritting shades the interior and reduces the glare on views to the outside. Along the upper level curbside where concrete would meet the curtainwall, openings are cut to introduce natural daylight into the baggage claim area and visually connect the two levels.

## Restrooms

Often an afterthought in airport design, RDU sets a new benchmark for restroom design. With innumerable changes in baggage policies, security screening and traveler demographics, the fundamental basics of restroom design are vastly different than they were even a decade ago. Today's travelers have more carry-ons, and, for security reasons, need to keep an ever-watchful eye on these bags. Passengers entering RDU's restrooms need navigate only one turn. Upon entering, the far wall is composed of floor-to-ceiling glass that bathes the restrooms in soft, natural light to enhance the aesthetics. Elongated stalls allow bags to easily fit inside them, and slightly tilted mirrors above the urinals keep bags in sight, even when behind their owners.

106

*Below:* Large-scale study model of ultimate development
*Facing page:* Elevation of ticketing hall wall with entry to restrooms and retail

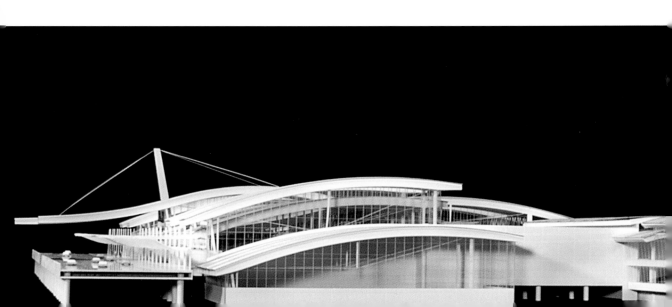

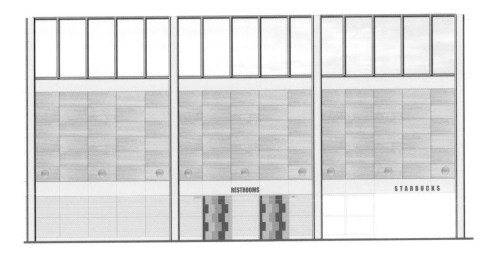

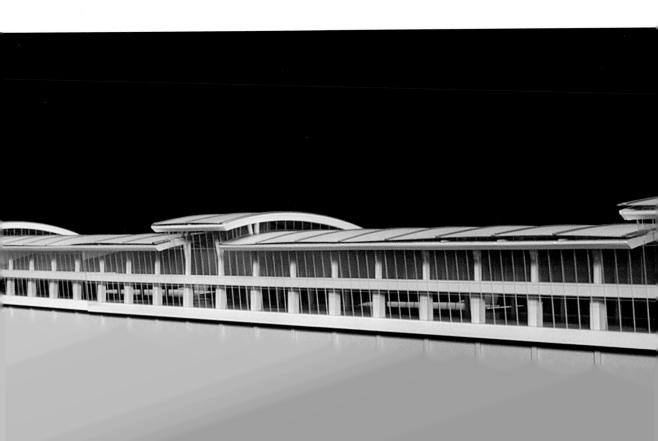

**Ceiling**

Made from state-of-the-art materials using cutting-edge technology, the roof's curvilinear forms and lenticular trusses pay homage not only to the area's rich past, but also its dynamic future.

The roof's abstracted rolling landscape and dynamic curbside canopies provide an informative and solid foundation for the artful weaving of materials, patterns, artwork, spatial relationships, and light and shadow into a cohesive and comfortable experience for airport customers.

*Right:* Early study model
*Facing page top left:* Basketmaker at the Poplar Grove Plantation
*Facing page top right:* Ceiling truss detail
*Facing page middle left:* Woodworker from the Hickory Chair Company
*Facing page middle right:* Ceiling truss detail
*Facing page bottom left:* Ceiling truss detail
*Facing page bottom right:* Ceiling truss detail

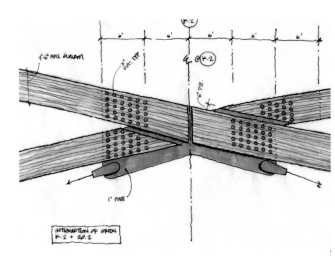

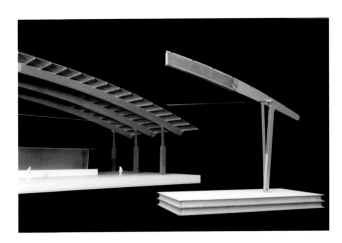

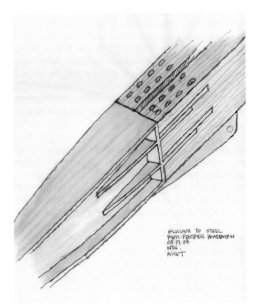

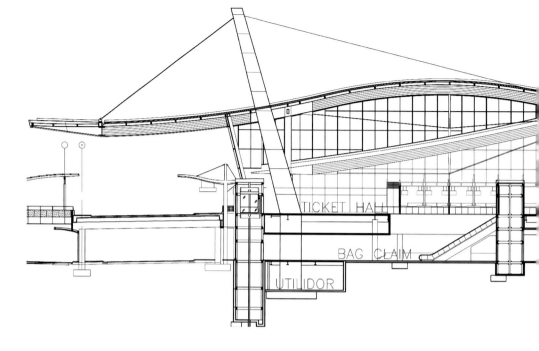

Within the image: TICKET HALL / BAG CLAIM / UTILIDOR

## Security

After checking in or arriving with a boarding pass already in hand, passengers enter through a single security checkpoint located just beyond the Great Hall's atrium. A sufficient number of stations are added during each phase of development, and several options are available should the need for increased stations arise. With arriving passengers passing by along the south side of security, this space remains very active, yet easily controlled. Past security, passengers emerge into a large composure area from which they can orient themselves before descending to the concourse by way of escalators, stairs, or a central elevator.

## Concessions

Most concessions are located along the concourse in hubs at junctures in the moving sidewalks. Each of these hubs features a diverse grouping of food, beverage, news, and retail outlets to ensure that patrons need not venture off their route in order to acquire the goods and services they seek. A variety of concessions are also provided pre-security so that well-wishers and meeters and greeters can access the concessions they desire, along with departing and arriving passengers.

## Public Art

With a concerted commission for the selection of public art at the onset of design, artists, architects, and the airport's authority worked together to identify and make ready designated locations throughout the facility for a wide variety of original art. Many, like the mosaics that detail the recessed portion of the restroom entry, have become part of the design, clearly illustrating the powerful contribution of art and architecture.

*Above:* Section from curbside through security to concourse
*Right:* Entrance to security

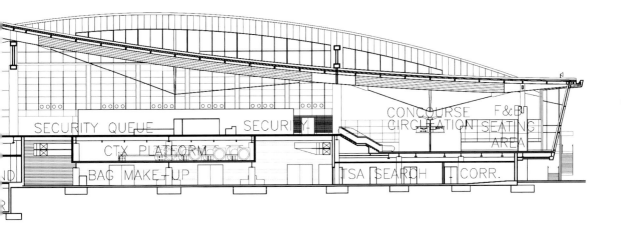

SECURITY QUEUE    SECURITY    CONCOURSE    F&B
                              CIRCULATION SEATING
                                   AREA

CTX PLATFORM

BAG MAKE-UP    TSA SEARCH    CORR.

## Airside Arrival Experience

Maintaining a consistent identity from ticketing to concourse, wooden lenticular trusses soar overhead at 30-foot (nine-meter) intervals. Carpet patterns and terrazzo flooring similar to that in the other areas of the terminal intuitively guide passengers from their gates to baggage claim. Also aiding them in their journey are moving sidewalks. Gate lounges are clustered to maximize views through the curtainwall to the airfield and to allow as much light as possible to wash the space. The curtainwall runs the full length of the concourse and caps its ends, further adding to the dynamism of the space.

## International Arrivals Experience

International arrivals deplane at the north end of the concourse where passengers can ascend via an escalator or elevator to a sterile, glass-enclosed corridor. In addition to its glass enclosure, the corridor lies 17 feet above ground to ensure adequate separation between international and domestic travelers. The corridor leads to passport control, the second step in the FIS screening process. Passport control is located on the upper level and between the concourse and landside terminal. Moving walkways aid corridor circulation.

## Bag Claim

The Central Atrium creates an experience equally exciting for arriving passengers as for those departing. This airy space takes arriving passengers down one flight to a lofty daylit baggage claim area where varied ceiling heights add an element of interest. BIDs are located just off the opening and, in a clear, large, and legible font, direct those claiming luggage to the appropriate carousel. Baggage offices, restrooms, and concessions provide those waiting with the services they desire, while taxis, passenger pick-up, and parking are outside, on the lower level of curbside.

*Left:* Concourse rendering detailing second-story international arrival
*Above:* Security and concourse juncture

# PEK

Terminal 3 & Concourses
Beijing International Airport

| | |
|---|---|
| location | Beijing, China |
| condition | new construction |
| type | multi-airline hub, O&D |
| area | 37,000,000 sqft (3,440,000 sqm) |
| annual pax | 60 million at capacity<br>*UD: 72 million* |
| gates | 75 attached & detached<br>*UD: 86* |
| scope | design competition entry |

*Previous page:*
Central Court

*Right:*
Circulation diagram

*Below:*
Model of ultimate
development

*Facing page:*
Site plan of ultimate
development

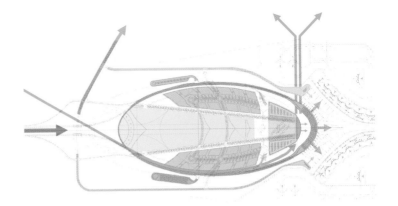

116

**Master Plan**

Since its completion in 1959, PEK has undergone a number of expansions with the latest occurring in 1999. That expansion targeted the airport's handling capacity, which was estimated to become 35 million passengers annually by 2005. With over 24 million passengers in 2001, and double-digit increases in 2002, actual growth is far outpacing anticipated growth and leading to an inevitable strain on capacity. This growing air passenger volume, along with numerous other issues, led airport operators and political officials to expand PEK with the addition of Terminal 3 (T3). Other issues that factored into the decision were: the need for greater operational flexibility, the need for a facility to serve as both an international and a domestic hub, and the need to increase non-airline revenue. Moreover, the 2008 Olympics necessitates an airport that is of the highest caliber in the world—a memorable gateway that succeeds as a representative of the region.

The landside terminal building is a three-level structure, with departures on the upper level and arrivals on the ground level. A basement level, fortified to withstand the site's high water table, houses baggage systems and the intra-airport APM. A mezzanine level, halfway between the arrivals and departures levels, is where passengers and visitors enter the building from the urban rail station and parking areas. The airside concourses attached to the terminal are designed exclusively for international arrivals and departures, while linear island concourses served by an APM provide service for all domestic passengers.

**Phasing**

PEK's overall capacity can increase from 35 million passengers a year to 60 million upon the completion of T3's Phase I, and grow to its ultimate development level of up to 72 million by 2020, with the addition of only six international gates and five domestic gates. On the international concourse, gates would be added at the two north piers with three aircraft at each pier. On the domestic concourses, the additional gates would be added to the second, most northerly remote concourse. Both expansion scenarios would be minimally disruptive because of their simplicity and operational convenience. The phased expansion for ultimate development of the terminal building's landside would be similarly efficient.

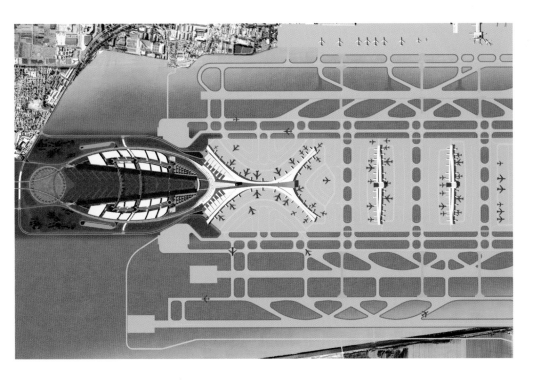

### Departure Experience

In the expansion plan, driving passengers exiting the Liang Ma Qiao Expressway and arriving at PEK are greeted via a system of internal roadways and curbsides arranged elliptically. The elliptical design is a well-defined and elegant foreground from which the terminal springs. The building is a sculpture, with a roof form that changes in heights, its ultimate apex as the building's center. The roof forms penetrate each other, while also lifting and peeling away. These juxtapositions introduce daylight into the building, as do walls of glass and clerestories. The composition accentuates the sense of movement through flight.

Visitors wishing travelers farewell enter off the curbside into a public space known as the well-wishers hall.

## Ticketing

International passengers check in on the east side of the building, while domestic passengers check in on the west. International travelers have additional stations for customs and plant and animal quarantine prior to entering the ticketing hall. Partially exposed steel trusses span the two large rooms in a pattern that opens the zone between the ticket islands and the clerestories above. The ceiling is sculpted with a gentle curve in plan that intuitively leads passengers from the center of the building to gate lounges.

Passengers find the appropriate ticket counter with the aid of electronic display systems suspended in front of each counter, indicating airline and flight information. The domestic and international ticketing halls accommodate five and seven ticket islands respectively, and each is equipped with 24 counters and many electronic ticketing stations.

After both domestic and international passengers proceed through the ticketing and baggage check-in areas, they embark on different routes to reach their respective concourses and departure gates.

## Security

For the domestic passenger, whose airplane gate is located on either Concourse B or C, the first stop after check-in is security, located in the domestic ticketing hall toward the center of the building. After clearing security, the domestic passenger descends via escalator or elevator to a train platform where they board an APM to the concourses.

For the international passenger, the first step after check-in is hygienic quarantine, passport control, and security, all located toward the center of the building. The checkpoints—separated into three groups to maximize flexibility—are located under the large and gently curving ceiling form. Upon leaving security, the international passenger is directed with signage to the appropriate gate.

## Central Court

At the center of the landside terminal building, on the upper level, a Central Court extends to the ground level. It is surrounded with walkways onto which retail and concession storefronts open. All visitors, prior to entering the domestic or international ticketing halls, have exposure to these revenue-generating businesses.

Stone paving introduces pattern and color while providing a lasting and low-maintenance walking surface; it also speaks to the exceptionally high quality of the building's materials. The structural columns that support the roof are finely finished, hand-rubbed, poured-in-place concrete. The structural steel braces and struts are clad in a refined metal finish, either stainless steel or aluminum. Their color is a soft reflective silver that enhances the modern quality of the architecture.

## Concessions

In the landside terminal, concessions are oriented around the aforementioned Central Court. However, as with most international airport terminals, the majority of airside revenue is generated by the international passenger. Therefore, the majority of the concession outlets are concentrated on the international departures level, grouped in zones that provide passengers with convenience and variety. For the domestic satellites, concessions are concentrated around the center core where all passengers arrive and depart.

## Arrival Experience

The ground level of the terminal building comprises the baggage claim and meeter and greeter area for both domestic and international passengers. In order to counterbalance this level's mandatory recess below grade, the design features exceptionally tall ceilings. The height creates an open, airy, and spacious environment.

The program requirements are logically arranged at this level so the domestic baggage claim is directly under the domestic check-in, and the international baggage claim is directly under the international check-in. After passengers claim their baggage from one of ten carousels, they proceed to the meeter and greeter area or to the ground transportation area.

## Sustainability

Numerable green building strategies are incorporated, including: selecting a brownfield site, choosing appropriate erosion and sediment control plans, incorporating mass transportation alternatives, reducing the heat island effect and light pollution, using water-efficient landscape design, utilizing innovative wastewater technologies, employing a comprehensive Building Systems Commissioning Plan, and providing on-site renewable energy opportunities. However, the greatest emphasis has been placed on resource efficiency. Major components of the exterior and the core of the building incorporate recycled steel, a high level of fly ash, and recycled aluminum, concrete, and asphalt. The interior of the building incorporates materials with high quantities of recycled materials and materials made of sustainable products.

*Page 118 top:* Departure level drop off
*Page 118 bottom:* Boy with an umbrella riding in a cart
*Page 119 top:* Ticketing hall
*Page 119 bottom:* Buildings at the Temple of Heaven
*Left top:* Concourse juncture with security
*Left bottom:* Bridge over Kunming Lake

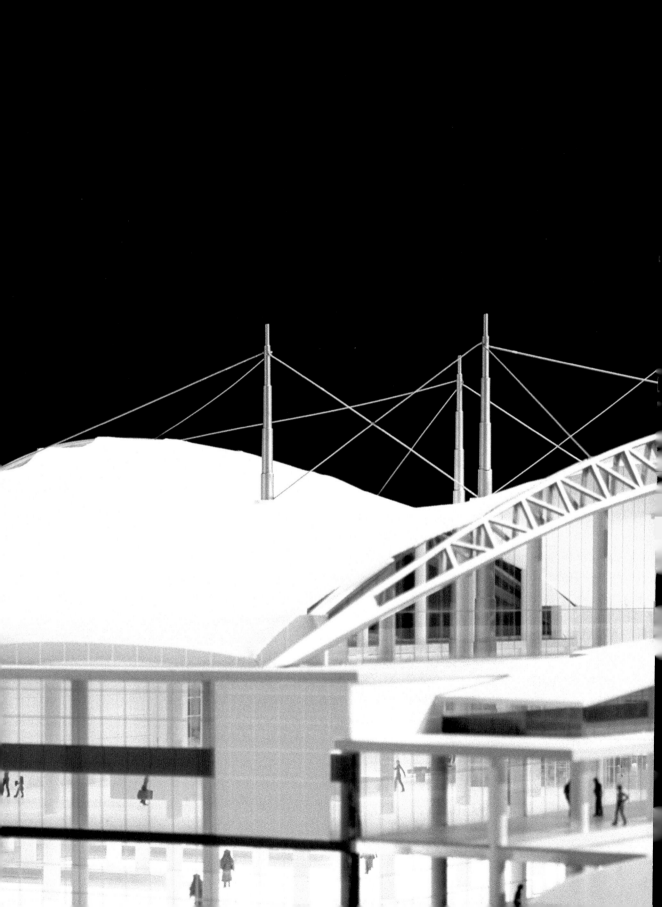

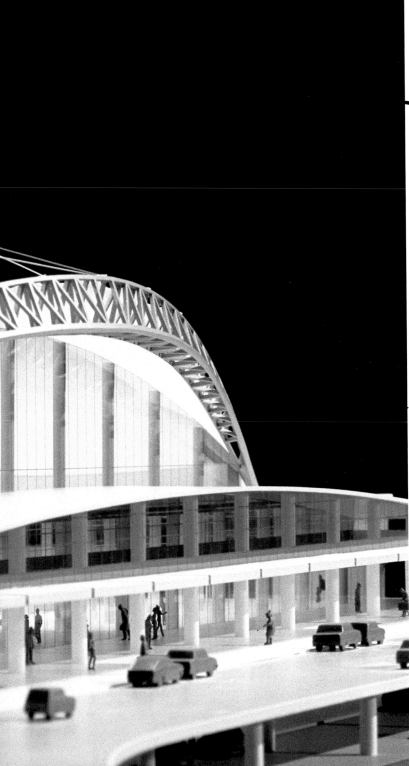

# TRV

Terminal & Concourse
Trivandrum International Airport

| | |
|---|---|
| location | Trivandrum, India |
| condition | new construction |
| type | multi-airline hub, O&D |
| area | 100,000 sqft (9,290 sqm) |
| | *UD: 400,000 sqft (37,160 sqm)* |
| annual pax | 1 million at capacity |
| | *UD: 10 million* |
| gates | 3 attached & detached |
| | *UD: 14* |
| scope | design competition entry |

*Previous page:* Departure curbside
*Below:* Section from curbside to concourse
*Right:* Site plan with designation for ultimate development

124

## Background

The city of Thiruvananathapuram, in the state of Kerala, was designated as one of *National Geographic Traveler* magazine's "50 Must See Destinations of a Lifetime." The sprawling city blankets seven hills along the southernmost portion of India's coastline. The city's name, literally translated as "the place of the sacred serpent," is a testament not only to the region's rolling topography, but also, more directly, to lords Anantha and Vishnu. Depicted in the local ancient temple of Padmanabhaswamy, Ananth is the serpent upon which Lord Vishnu reclines comfortably and in godly glory. Additional points of interest for Thiruvananathapuram's healthy tourism base are the pervasive Kerala-style architecture of tiled roofs and carved gables, a well-regarded botanic gardens, a zoo with its quaint museum, and of course, the lively intellectual community.

## Master Plan

Three gates located in two nearly obsolete terminals have served the 52 annual flights into TRV. Air India, Gulf Air, and Kuwait Airways top the list of carriers serving this tropical paradise. With passenger numbers rising and increasing interest in the region, Airports Authority of India sought concept designs and suggested revisions to the airport's existing master plan. Best described as indeterminate, the existing master plan called for little more than new development to be located opposite the existing runways on part of the site's 583 acres accessible by established roadways.

Given the relatively small air traffic volume with incremental growth forecasted for the foreseeable future, a two-story linear terminal complex was proposed that would accommodate both north and south modularized expansion. Each module would provide ticketing, baggage, and gate facilities required to service up to three aircrafts simultaneously.

SITE PLAN

SCALE = 1:1000

## Departure Experience

From curbside inward, the departing passenger experiences a facility that is sheltered by the translucent materials of fabric and glass. The weatherproof materials protect against monsoons, while reducing heat build-up during summer months. These translucent building materials also help orient passengers through the departure experience, while imbuing the facility with a sense

DEPARTURE LEVEL PLAN
SCALE = 1:200

Hold Room

Concourse

Retail/Service

Offices

Security

Ticketing Hall

LOUNGE

Ticketing Hall

Inspection

Inspection

Well Wishers Hall

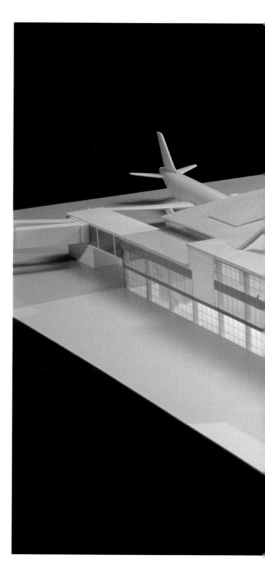

*Above left:* Departure level floor plan
*Above:* Aerial of departure level curbside

of calm and cleanliness. From curbside, passengers can visually orient themselves to ticket counters, from which they can locate security, and, ultimately, retail, and boarding lounges.

The largest portion of TRV's passengers are tourists, and travelers tend to arrive at airports with ample time to shop, eat, and relax before boarding their plane. This design supports the tourism bureau's economic viewpoint that it is essential to perpetuate the relaxing holiday experience, so that vacationers will have positive last impressions of Kerala and India. A relaxing, enjoyable environment is equally important from the airport operators' economic perspective. Passengers who are relaxed and anticipate a good airport experience, tend to arrive early and therefore patronize the concessions, which bolsters TRV's revenue.

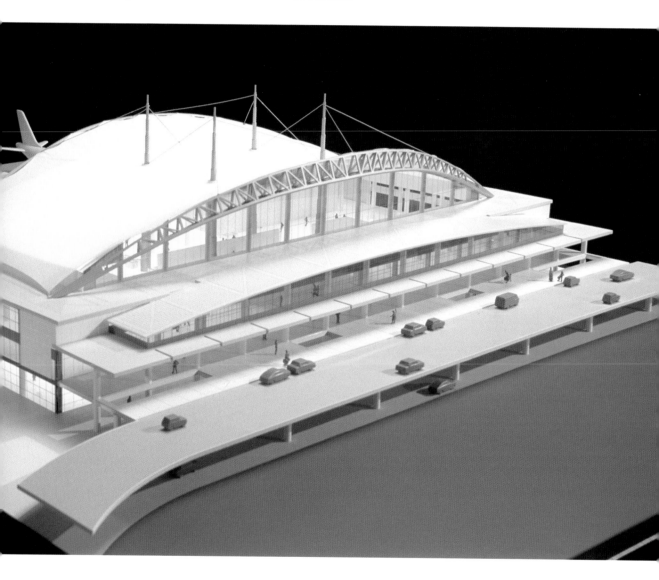

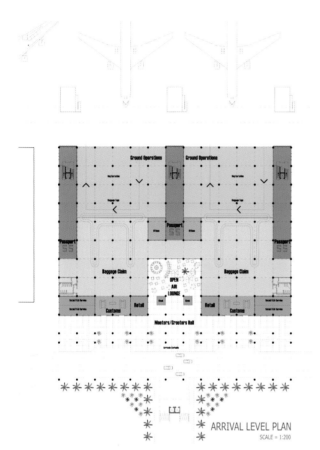

ARRIVAL LEVEL PLAN
SCALE = 1:200

*Below left:* Arrival level floor plan
*Bottom:* Houseboat on the backwaters of Alleppey in Kerala
*Facing page top:* Ticketing hall
*Facing page bottom:* Concourse elevation

## Arrival Experience

TRV embodies and exudes the essence of India, though, more specifically, Kerala's rich geography. Phoenicians, Romans, Arabs, Chinese, and Western Europeans are among the groups that have had the most enduring impact on Kerala's culture and built environment. From religion to building materials, it is this amalgam of influences that served as the primary inspiration for the airport's architecture.

The upswept, anticlastic roof form recalls among other images the curvaceous lines of an elephant, bowed houseboat canopies, and arched mosque and temple arcades. In fact, TRV's strong, rhythmically placed interior columns pay further homage to the arcades in that they not only support the roof form, they also define circulation patterns. Similarly, the grid produced by the fabric roof's cable-stay structure is an intentional tribute to the traditional ceilings of houseboats, a solution that is at once aesthetically pleasing and functional. And yet, the symbolism goes further. The state-of-the-art materials and technologies necessary to bring this design to fruition also speak of India and Kerala's future at the forefront of global industry.

Test flight of 1902 Wright glider

Inauguration of the Pan-American Terminal at Miami in 1929

LaGuardia Airport circa 1950

# Airport Architecture: Evolution and Beyond

By Curtis Worth Fentress, FAIA & Thomas J. Walsh, AIA

When the Wright brothers launched the first flying machine at Kitty Hawk, North Carolina, on December 17, 1903, little did they dream of the culture their invention would generate. Over the last century, airplanes gave rise to airports, which began as little more than sheds appended to hangars. Today, these facilities are economic engines and initiators of air-based cities, or *aerotropolises*. In order to fully understand this building type and its signature element—the terminal—one must understand its history.

The airport terminal, as a concept, was born in 1926 when airline operators needed facilities in which to queue and shelter waiting passengers. Built in 1928, Miami's Pan American Terminal is an existing example of the first terminal type, which was then called a depot.

As popularity for commercial air travel grew, so did the need for space and more importantly, a means to create convenient, functional, and symbolic gateways. Architects of this era, beginning in 1929, translated train stations into air stations as they sought to embody the gateway ideal and provide linkage to the central business districts they served. New York's LaGuardia Airport was developed during this time and, notwithstanding numerous modernizations, remains an example of both the successes and shortcomings of this translation.

From 1945 onward, some of the shortcomings from the previous era were addressed. For example, the TWA terminal at Kennedy Airport in New York and the Charles de Gaulle Airport in Paris employ "international-style" architecture as a means to express, in static form, the essence of flight. Sky-bound forms and spacious interiors characterize these terminals as well as their contemporaries. Additionally, during this period the rectilinear plan

was developed and implemented to better process passenger check-in, boarding, and baggage claim operations.

Until 1959, airport passenger functions operated largely out of a single, expansion-prohibitive facility. This approach became antiquated when airports like Midway in Chicago began processing annual passengers in excess of ten million. With forecasted exponential growth, airport planners of this era implemented a configuration at Chicago's O'Hare that separated the terminal from concourse operations—that is, disconnected landside from airside operations. This division has remained a constant in airport development, particularly as a means to aid expansion.

Since 1973, airports worldwide have embraced concessions as a major source of non-airline revenue. In doing so, they have sought to acquire and employ advancements in technology. From full-scale shopping facilities to wireless internet

access, the lucrative nature of concessions continues unbounded. Munich may be considered the first international airport to fully capitalize on these opportunities, but airports like Seattle-Tacoma, Baltimore, and Heathrow are taking advantage in smaller, yet similarly unique and memorable ways.

Of course, the most evolving design driver is security. Security mandates were first implemented with fortitude following the rash of hijackings from 1968 to 1972. The U.S. and 49 other nations signed the Hague Convention, which led to the introduction of metal detectors. While there were numerous minor changes over the years, it wasn't until the September 11, 2001, terrorist attacks that security mandates radically changed again. Not only have queue times at security checkpoints increased, so has the need for larger boarding lounges, supplementary post-security concessions, and reinvented well-wisher and meeter-and-greeter halls.

For each evolution in airport architecture—from sheltering awaiting passengers to creating a gateway, linking to the local business district, embodying the essence of flight, streamlining processes, providing for expansion, offering amenities, and securing the experience—the characteristic and inventive solution was precipitated by a need for change. As the word "evolution" suggests, the eras operate as

a collection: each new solution builds upon the solid foundation of those before it.

And yet, there is more. Extensive research, constant travel, and over 25 years of experience on numerous airport projects has taught us additional strategies for the creation of successful, long-term facilities. We know that cost-consciousness is a virtue, as are longevity, flexibility, wayfinding, and the seamless incorporation of multimodal transportation networks. We also know that reflective architecture is influential architecture, for, as Winston Churchill explained, "we shape our buildings, and afterwards our buildings shape us[1]."

## Cost-consciousness

Cost-consciousness involves more than just respecting a project's budget. It also means making

---

**1** "On the night of May 10, 1941, with one of the last bombs of the last serious raid, our House of Commons was destroyed by the violence of the enemy, and we have now to consider whether we should build it up again, and how, and when. We shape our buildings, and afterwards our buildings shape us. Having dwelt and served for more than forty years in the late Chamber, and having derived very great pleasure and advantage therefrom, I, naturally, should like to see it restored in all essentials to its old form, convenience and dignity."
—WSC, 28 October 1943 to the House of Commons
(meeting in the House of Lords).

material selections based on prudent life-cycle and replacement cost analysis. From building systems to exterior and interior finishes, all elements of a terminal's architecture should provide maximum benefit at minimum cost on a macro level. This means devising solutions like wrapping the lower portion of columns in public spaces with brushed stainless steel panels that will mask the blemishes luggage carts leave behind. It could also mean specifying granite or terrazzo flooring in only the most high trafficked areas, while using low-cost, durable carpets in less trafficked zones and those in need of noise dampening. Prioritization and innovative solutions lie at the heart of every cost-conscious decision, and often yield some of the most brilliant solutions.

## Longevity

Life-cycle and replacement cost analysis touch on the issue of longevity. Yet, longevity is not restricted to durability. It can also be defined as the endurance or permanence of a structure, or its continuing relevance. Terminals that exude permanence and

durability defy being designated as outdated. Some achieve this by encapsulating a period in time deemed worthy of remembering, while others do so by being flexible and adaptable—capable of weathering innumerable changes. These two categories are not mutually exclusive. When done well, airports should not only epitomize the achievements of their era, but also provide the foundation for future advancements.

## Flexibility

Creating spaces that can adapt to future needs generally means designing expansion phases to take the facility through the next 50 years, or two to three times its current passenger load. While there is an understanding of the technologies that may be implemented in the next decade, nothing is certain. Furthermore, it is impossible to plan for the effects of innovations like the internet or for requirements as a result of tragic events like September 11th. During planning and design phases, designers must question how the airport could react if any of its various building elements became obsolete or

needed to be significantly expanded. Whatever the scenario, the answer always centers on adaptation. Whether arranging ticketing halls to house any combination of linear, island, and kiosk counters, or modularizing concourses to accommodate fluctuations in the number of concession and gate lounges offered, each space must maximize adjacency and infrastructure efficiency.

### Wayfinding

Positive passenger experiences begin with intuitive navigation. A primary challenge in airport design is keeping complex projects from becoming a maze in their attempt to fulfill all of the functional needs. Successful solutions begin with a comfortable scale and a clear plan. Travelers and visitors need to know at a glance where to enter, and, once inside, they should be directed with a minimum of graphics. They should also be given a moment of repose, to tell them they have arrived, to make them feel greeted, and to explain how the building works. We call this process "discovering the natural order," and often it entails stacking arrival and departure levels, placement of all ticketing counters immediately inside arrival doors, spacious zones for retail and security, and location of baggage carrousels as close to the departure doors as possible.

### Multimodal Transportation Network

Airports should not only be planned for internal circulation, they should also be planned as major elements in the creation of efficient and effective multimodal transportation networks for cities and regions. Planners should focus on reducing congestion through the thoughtful incorporation of adequate and appropriately located space for arriving and departing rail and subway lines, buses, taxis, and personal vehicles. These spaces should flow naturally into the building's internal circulation system to alleviate stress on the check-in and baggage claim stations. A reduction in the number of long-term parking spaces encourages travelers to utilize mass transit, while an increase in the number of spaces for greeters encourages patronization of the airport's retail facilities.

### Reflective architecture

First impressions are lasting impressions. The design and feel of an airport conveys how a community views itself and the value it places on newcomers. Well-developed and consistent design elements that reference local geography serve to brand and promote the airport and region. Striking vernacular designs often become regional landmarks and icons, which consistently appear in print and television media seeking to capture the essence of place. From airlines to retail outlets, corporations, educational institutions, convention and tourism boards, and local citizens, the airport and its surrounding community benefit from attention garnered by iconic design. As a city gains a heightened reputation through significant architectural statements, it becomes a more attractive place to visit, relocate to, and take pride in as a citizen.

Fentress Bradburn Architects gained distinction in the field of airport design with the opening of Denver International Airport's Passenger Terminal Complex in 1995. Denver's terminal has been lauded as "a global attraction" by Colorado Governor William Owen, noted as having the "nicest architecture" of American airports by the *Wall Street Journal* and recognized as the "best run airport in America" by *Time* magazine. Its design and technological innovations continue to be the subject of lectures and publications as the terminal remains the largest fabric-enclosed structure in America. And yet, fabric architecture does not define Fentress Bradburn Architects. Instead, the firm continues to define landmark airports the world over that grow out of a concrete understanding of the past, a comprehensive approach to contemporary and future needs, and a design philosophy that yields ambassadorial designs. ∎

*Facing page:*
Departure of Boeing
777 at DEN

# Credits

## DEN

**Passenger Terminal Complex**
**Denver International Airport**
Denver, Colorado, USA
1994

**Client:** City and County of Denver

**Architect, Interior Design:**
Fentress Bradburn Architects
**Associate Architect:** Pouw and Associates;
Bertram A. Bruton and Associates

**Acoustic:** Shen Milson & Wilke;
David L. Adams Associates
**Baggage, BIDS, FIDS, Signage:** TRA
**Civil Engineer:** Martin/Martin; HDR
**Codes, Life Safety:** Rolf Jensen & Associates
**Cost Estimator:** Western Industrial Contractors
**Curtainwall:** Heitmann & Associates
**Daylighting:** Architectural Energy Corporation;
LightForms Engineers
**Electrical Engineer:** Black & Veatch;
Riegel Associates; Roos Szynskie
**Food Service:** Thomas Ricca Associates
**Geotechnical Engineer:** CTL/Thompson
**Graphic Design:** TKD Designs
**Landscape:** Pouw and Associates
**Lighting:** H.M. Brandston & Partners; LAM Partners
**Mechanical Engineer:** Abeyta Engineering
Consultants; Black & Veatch; Riegel Associates
**Parking:** Carl Walker Engineers
**Security:** Aerospace Services International
**Structural Engineer:** S.A. Miro; Severud
Associates with Horst Berger; Martin/Martin

**Vertical Transportation:**
Hesselberg Keese & Associates
**Wind, Snow Loads:**
Rowan Williams Davies & Irwin

## BKK

**Terminal & Concourse**
**Second Bangkok International Airport**
Bangkok, Thailand
Design 1993

**Client:** Airport Authority of Thailand

**Architect, Interior Design:**
Fentress Bradburn Architects

**Planning, Civil, Building System Engineer:**
McClier Aviation Group

## DOH

**Terminal & Concourse; Support Buildings;**
**Control Tower**
**Doha International Airport**
Doha, Qatar
Design 1998; 1999; Design 2001

**Client:** Ministry of Municipal Affairs and
Agriculture

**Architect, Interior Design:**
Fentress Bradburn Architects

**Airport Planning:** Landrum & Brown
**Aircraft Systems, Communication, Baggage:** Swanson Rink
**Civil, Structural, Mechanical, Electrical Engineer:** Dar Al-Handasah
**Concessions:** Sypher Mueller
**Control Tower, Fueling Systems:** Aarotec
**Mechanical Peer Review:**
Riegel Doyle Associates
**Quantity Surveyors:** Westbury + Northcrofts
**Signage and Graphic Design:**
Monigle Associates
**Specifications:** Carpenter Associates
**Structural Peer Review:** Martin/Martin

# JCN

**Terminal & Concourse**
**Incheon International Airport**
Incheon Bay, Seoul, Republic of Korea
2000

**Client:** Korean Airport Construction Authority

**Design Architect:** Fentress Bradburn Architects
**Architect of Record:** Korean Architects
Collaborative International (KACI) a consortium
of Baum Architects Engineers Consultants, Hi-Lim
Architects & Engineers, Jung-Lim Architects &
Engineers and Wondoshi Architects
**Interior Design:** Fentress Bradburn Architects;
KACI with Forum Design; J.M. Wilmotte

**Acoustical:** Shen Milsom & Wilke
**Baggage:** BNP
**Building Maintenance:** Citadel Consulting
**Civil Engineer:** Sevan Engineer
**Code, Life Safety:** Rolf Jensen & Associates
**Concession:** Sypher Mueller International;
Crang and Boake
**Curtainwall:** Heitmann & Associates
**Electrical Engineer:** Fine E&C
**Fire Protection Engineer:**
Korea Fire Protection Engineering; Swanson Rink
**Landscape:** Seo-Ahn Landscape Architects; Civitas
**Lighting Design:** LAM Partners; Kookje Lighting
**Mechanical, Electrical, Telecommunication:**
McClier Corporation; Swanson Rink
**Mechanical Engineer:**
Han-Il Mechanical Engineering Consultant
**People Mover:** Lea + Elliott
**Specifications:** Carpenter Associates
**Structural Engineer:** Martin/Martin;
Sen-Structural Engineers; Jeon and Associates
**Vertical Transportation:**
Lerch Bates & Associates
**Wind Tunnel:** Rowan Williams Davies & Irwin

# TFS

**Terminal & Concourse**
**Reina Sofia International Airport**
Tenerife-Sur, Canary Islands, Spain
Design 1999

**Client:** AENA

**Architect, Interior Design:**
Fentress Bradburn Architects
**Associate Architect:**
Correa & Estevez, Arquitectos

**Airfield Planning, Site, Building Engineer:**
GHESA

**Cable Supported Glass Wall:**
Advanced Structures
**Civil Engineer:** Rosewater Engineering
**Code Consultant:** Bob Pielow Associates
**Concession, Food Service:**
Sypher Mueller International; Leigh Fisher Associates
**Cost Estimator:** KJM Associates
**Electrical Engineer:** Sparling
**Geotechnical Engineer:** Civiltech Corporation
**Landscape:** Don Shimono Associates
**Lighting:** LAM Partners
**Mechanical, Plumbing Engineer:**
Wood/Harbinger
**Signage, Graphic Design:** Andrew R. Goulding
**Specifications:** Carpenter Associates
**Structural Engineer:**
Anderson Bjornstad, Kane Jacobs

# SEA

**Central Terminal Redevelopment**
**Seattle-Tacoma International Airport**
Seattle, Washington USA
2005

**Client:** Port of Seattle

**Architect, Interior Design:**
Fentress Bradburn Architects
**Associate Architect:**
Streeter & Associates Architects

**Acoustical Consultant:** The Greenbusch Group
**Baggage, FIDS, Security:** URS/Greiner

# MUC

**Terminal 2**
**Munich International Airport**
Munich, Germany
Design 1998

**Client:** Munich Airport Authority

**Architect:** Fentress Bradburn Architects

# RDU

**Terminal C & Concourse Redevelopment**
**Raleigh-Durham International Airport**
Raleigh, North Carolina USA
2008

**Client:** Raleigh-Durham Airport Authority

**Architect:** Fentress Bradburn Architects
**Associate Architect:** O'Brien Atkins Associates;
The Freelon Group
**Interior Design:** Compositions,
Fentress Bradburn Architects

**Acoustic:** Cerami & Associates
**Aircraft Systems:** AERO Systems Engineering
**Baggage:** BNP Associates
**Civil Engineer:** URS Corporation;
TY LIN International
**Construction Manager:** Parsons
**Cost Estimator:** Handscomb Faithful & Gould
**Curtainwall:** Heitmann & Associates
**Geotechnical Engineer:** GeoTecnologies; Tierra
**FIDS, BIDS, IT:** URS Corporation
**Landscape:** HadenStanziale
**Life Safety & Codes:** Rolf Jensen & Associates
**Lighting:** LAM Partners
**Mechanical Electrical, Fire Protection,**
**Plumbing Engineer:** ARUP; RMF Engineering
**Parking Garage Consultant:** Walker Parking
**Quantity Surveyors:** KCI Associates of N.C.
**Security:** Kroll Security Services Group
**Signage:** Apple Designs
**Structural Engineer:** ARUP; Stewart Engineering

**Vertical, Horizontal Transport:**
Lerch Bates & Associates
**Wind, Snow Analysis:**
Roan Williams Davies & Irwin

# PEK

**Terminal 3 & Concourses**
**Beijing International Airport**
Beijing, China
Design 2002

**Client:** Beijing International Airport Group
Corporation

**Architect:** Fentress Bradburn Architects

**Airfield Planning:** Parsons
**Civil, Structural, Mechanical, Electrical,**
**Plumbing, Fire Protection Engineer:** Parsons
**Baggage, Simulations:** Swanson Rink
**Automated People Mover:** Lea Elliot

# TRV

**Terminal & Concourse**
**Trivandrum International Airport**
Thiruvananathapuram, Kerala, India
Design 2003

**Client:** Airport Authority of India

**Architect:** Fentress Bradburn Architects
**Associate Architect:** C.P. Kurkreja Associates

# Photo Credits

Ellen Jaskol: 10

Fentress Bradburn Architects: 3, 12, 19, 22, 23, 35, 39, 40, 41, 50, 51, 55, 57, 60, 69, 72, 76, 77, 85, 88, 89, 90, 91, 92, 93, 94, 95, 96, 97, 100, 104, 105, 107, 108, 109, 110, 111, 112, 113, 116, 117, 124, 125, 126, 128, 129

Nick Merrick/Hedrich Blessing: Front Cover, Flap, 6, 15, 16, 21, 56, 57, 58, 62, 79, 80, 81, 82, 83, 87, 132, 142, Back Cover

Timothy Hursley: Flap, 4, 12, 14, 17, 18, 20

Carl Dalio: 25, 26, 28, 34, 36, 42, 43, 44, 45, 47, 114, 118, 119, 120, 129

Ron Johnson: 30, 31, 32, 44, 66, 71, 72, 78, 122, 127

Jeff Goldberg/Esto: Flap, 8, 48, 52, 53, 54, 59, 61, 63, 65, 131, 133

James P. Scholz: 74, 84, 85, 86, 87

Jason A. Knowles: 103, 106, 109

Stanley Doctor: 51, 55, 98, 100

The Denver Post/Brian Brainerd: 135

The Seattle Times: 77

LAM Partners: 103, 111

Corbis: 13, 34, 52, 119, 130

Bill Ross/Corbis: 13

Bettmann/Corbis: 31, 130

Charles E. Rotkin/Corbis: 31

Macduff Everton/Corbis: 33, 120

Christine Osborne/Corbis: 41

Bojan Brecelj/Corbis: 42

Tim de Waele/Corbis: 46

Bohemian Nomad Picturemakers/Corbis: 54

Carmen Redondo/Corbis: 63

Diego Lezama Orezzoli/Corbis: 68

Despotovic Dusko/Corbis Sygma: 68

John Carter/Corbis: 70

Robert Holmes/Corbis: 70

Jose F. Poblete/Corbis: 73

Vauthey Pierre/Corbis Sygma: 73

Bossu Regis/Corbis Sygma: 91, 96

Massimo Listri/Corbis: 93

Adam Woolfitt/Corbis: 94

Ron Watts/Corbis: 102

David Muench/Corbis: 102

Michael Boys/Corbis: 104

Brownie Harris/Corbis: 109

Wally McNamee/Corbis: 118

Chris Lisle/Corbis: 128

# Glossary

**APM**: Automated People Mover

**ATCT**: Air Traffic Control Tower

**BID**: Baggage Information Display

**CBP**: Bureau of Customs and Border Protection

**CRT**: Cathode Ray Tube (display)

**FID**: Flight Information Display

**FIS**: Federal Inspection Service

**LED**: Light Emitting Diode (display)

**O&D**: Origin and Destination (non-hub)

**PAX**: Passenger(s)

**PHS**: Public Health Service

**RJ**: Regional Jet

**TSA**: Transportation Safety Administration

**UD**: Ultimate Development

**USFWS**: United States Fish and Wildlife Service

# Acknowledgements

Architecture is not created in a vacuum; it takes
a team. Fentress Bradburn Architects has enjoyed
the support of many people over the years—from
clients to consultants, contractors, product suppliers,
manufacturers, and more. Yet, the firm's greatest
support has come from its staff. The success
Fentress Bradburn enjoys today is a direct result of
the tremendous contributions of time, effort, and
creativity put forth by these people. Whether a
veteran principal or a summer intern, over the last
25 years the firm's staff has explored and advanced
the firm's mission: to produce exceptional, regional-
contextual architecture.

This book was also a team effort. Special thanks
are due to Jessica del Pilar who authored the
project descriptions. Additional thanks go to
Jennifer Fonseca, Karen Gilbert, Ned Kirschbaum,
Jason Knowles, Mark Outman, Tom Theobald, and
Thomas Walsh.

—Curtis Worth Fentress, FAIA

*Left:* Observation capabilities restored at SEA

First published in the United States of America by
Edizioni Press, Inc.
469 West 21st Street New York, New York 10011
www.edizionipress.com

ISBN: 1-931536-56.2
Library of Congress Catalogue Card Number: 2005936187

Printed in China

Design: Andrew Sloat
Editor: Sarah Palmer
Editorial Assistant: Nancy Sul

*Front Cover:* Bi-directionally curved curtainwall at SEA with views
to airfield
*Back Cover Top:* South-end curtainwall at DEN
*Back Cover Middle:* Curbside at JCN
*Back Cover Bottom:* Pacific Marketplace at SEA